hard men of WELSH RUGBY

hard men of WELSH RUGBY

LYNN DAVIES

y Lolfa

My thanks to Clive Rowlands for writing the Foreword to this book, and for his valuable comments with regard to the players I have included.

My thanks also to Derec Owen for his assistance.

First impression: 2011

The publishers wish to acknowledge the support of
Cyngor Llyfrau Cymru

Cover design: Y Lolfa
Cover photo: Media Wales
Photographs: Huw Evans Agency,
pages 18, 25, 33, 38, 44, 54, 60, 68, 78, 84, 104, 110, 119, 136.

Every attempt was made to ascertain
and contact the source of all the photographs in this book.

ISBN: 978 1 84771 352 0

FSC

Published and printed in Wales
on paper from well maintained forests by
Y Lolfa Cyf., Talybont, Ceredigion SY24 5HE
e-mail ylolfa@ylolfa.com
website www.ylolfa.com
tel 01970 832 304
fax 832 782

Hard Men

Foreword

IN RECENT YEARS much has been made of the fact that rugby has become physically harder. Yet it does not necessarily follow, of course, that participants of the game today are representative of a harder breed of player. Indeed during my involvement with the Wales team over many years, as a player, coach, manager and selector (a period which for the most part corresponds with the timespan of this book), I often came across players whose reputation as 'hard' men would even today be unsurpassed. These were men who, irrespective of size, were totally committed, who 'took no prisoners', who unstintingly made their physical presence felt on the field of play and who generally possessed a mental toughness that usually came with a 'never say die' philosophy. All this they usually accomplished within the laws of the game but were not averse, as the need arose, to resort to confrontational or clandestine action to counter unjust intimidation or unfair provocation from unprincipled opponents!

Many 'hard men' have represented Wales over the years and I'm sure Lynn Davies had difficulty in limiting his choice to just twenty players. Yet they form a truly representative cross section of the hard men I had cause to admire during my rugby career. In addition, their exceptional skills ensured that admiration was always coupled with immense pleasure.

Clive Rowlands
Wales National Team Coach, 1968–74

Introduction

IN RECENT YEARS the game of rugby union has undergone fundamental changes, the most significant of which was the advent of professional rugby in 1995. Players who were part of the first-class rugby scene were now expected to be super fit athletes displaying improved levels of speed, durability and power. In due course such developments became necessary, in order to meet with rugby's progression from being a 'contact' sport to a 'collision' sport. Adaptations to the ways in which the game has been played of late have also resulted in the nurturing of bigger, stronger and faster players in all positions. Consequently, clubs and international teams make use of a variety of conditioning experts to ensure that their teams are not found wanting in facets of the game that require such attributes. The regrettable consequence of such enhancements in modern rugby is a marked increase in the number of serious injuries sustained by players at the highest level.

Such uniformity of physicality has resulted, however, in a certain equalization of player prowess. For example, the strong men who line up against each other in a match situation often cancel each other out because their physique has been developed to a similar extent and in a like manner. As a result, it is the task of the coach to come up with better techniques and more penetrative tactics to ensure a team's superiority.

It is not often these days that players stand out purely

because of their physical attainments on the field. It could be argued that during the pre-professional period the opposite was true. During that time players were often a source of admiration because they were 'hard'. This implied that they displayed a particular brand of physical play which was of great benefit to the team. It could take many forms: being unflinching in aggressive areas of the game, such as in the turmoil of forward play, being fearless in the tackle or under the high ball, being immune to taking a backward step in conflict, being prepared to put one's body on the line for the sake of the team and being skilled in the art of surreptitious retribution when one's team was deemed to have suffered as a result of some evil deed perpetrated by the opposing team.

Of course 'hard' players were credited with such accomplishments without being able to draw upon the benefits of the intense preparation provided by the fitness and coaching gurus in the modern game. They did, however, have certain advantages over their modern counterparts. In days of old they could often go quietly about their business without fear of being seen by the referee. Today, there is every chance that they would have been spotted by one of the many refereeing officials, or picked up by one of many television cameras. The charismatic image which often accompanied their cavalier approach to the game was frequently enhanced by the spilling of blood whilst undertaking a particular act of bravado. Playing on with bloodied and unbowed commitment often resulted in greater admiration of the 'hard man'. The modern player is not able to draw upon such adulation, in that once bleeding occurs, the player concerned is wisely required to leave the field for treatment.

One of the many definitions of the word 'hard' provided by a reputable modern English dictionary is: *toughened by, or as if by, physical labour.* It is not surprising therefore that many 'hard' players of old relied upon the demands of their employment, for example the traditional coal and steel industries, to provide them with the strength, toughness and durability required on the rugby field. Other definitions of the word include:

firm or rigid, not easily dented or crushed

showing or requiring considerable physical or mental energy

inflicting pain, sorrow distress or hardship

Such descriptions seem so fitting when applied to many of the 'hard' men who became established in the Wales team, and who gave rugby followers so much pleasure, between 1945 and the inception of the professional era in 1995. This volume hopes to recall some of that pleasure. Yet there are so many other names that could easily have been included in the following pages and it is unfortunate that the likes of Clive Burgess, Terry Cobner, Norman Gale, Arthur Lewis, Barry Llewellyn, Rhys Stephens and Denzil Williams had to be omitted from this collection.

Lynn Davies
September 2011

JOHN BEVAN

JOHN C BEVAN, the Cardiff, Wales, Barbarians and British Lions rugby union three-quarter, was described by J P R Williams as "undoubtedly the strongest wing I have ever seen". He was born in Llwynypia in 1950 and raised in Tylorstown. While a pupil at Ferndale Grammar School, he was selected three times for Wales at under-15 level as a Number 8 and played five times for the Wales under-19 team as a winger. He became a student at Cardiff College of Education and regularly turned out for the college team. However, during this period he also joined Cardiff Rugby Club for whom he played 35 times, scoring 25 tries.

In 1971, at the age of 20 years 3 months, he was awarded his first full cap against England and scored a try as Wales won 22–6. He went on to play rugby union for his country on nine other occasions and at the end of his first Five Nations competition in 1971, he was selected to tour Australia and New Zealand with the British Lions, where he made a dramatic contribution as a prolific try scorer.

During that time, having touched down on 17 occasions in New Zealand, he equalled the try-scoring record on a Lions tour set by the legendary Irish winger, Tony O'Reilly. This total included four tries in the match against the celebrated Wellington team. Indeed during the early part of that tour, it appeared that he would easily break the Irishman's record, for J C had scored eleven tries in his first four games. As a result, he was selected to play

in the first Test against the All Blacks but, following a dip in form during the middle part of the tour, he lost his place to David Duckham for the remainder of the Test series.

The renowned Irish forward, Ray McLoughlin, was originally a first-choice prop for that series, before being ruled out through injury following a particularly dirty game against Canterbury. As a result he was given the responsibility of coaching the forwards by Carwyn James, the Lions coach. McLoughlin formed the opinion that John Bevan was stronger than half the Lions forwards and had the required attributes to hold his own in the front row.

This had been appropriately illustrated in that particular game against Canterbury, when, on one occasion, his path to the try line was seemingly blocked by three sturdy defenders. In the opinion of many observers on the day, J C took it upon himself to drive through all three and touch down in the corner in a manner which no other winger at the time could have accomplished. That try was replicated by J C in 1973, when he played for the Barbarians in that unforgettable game against the All Blacks. Receiving the ball some 20 metres out, he galloped for the try line and somehow succeeded in handing-off three would-be tacklers to ground the ball in the corner.

Those two memorable scores epitomised John Bevan's style and forte and his penchant for using brute force to get the better of opponents. He was a player who preferred to run through defenders, often deploying a powerful hand-off to very good effect, as opposed to running around them or resorting to a sidestep or a chip ahead. J P R Williams, who was also a member of that Lions tour to New Zealand, when referring to John Bevan's contribution, some years later, said: "It seems amazing that he didn't get seriously injured during the tour, but I suppose that reinforces my belief that the harder you go into a tackle the less likely you are to get hurt."

J C's muscular 6'0" and 13 stone frame exuded power and aggression and, coupled with a dogged determination and persistence, his fearless style would often cause panic amongst the opposition. When required, he could also cover ground with considerable speed and took great delight in harrying opponents when they were in possession. Often his appearance, in addition to his style of play, suggested an all-action, no nonsense approach, with his socks rolled down to his ankles, his sleeves rolled up and his raised clenched fist salute upon scoring a try (a custom he adopted after going north), all of which belied his essentially shy disposition.

It is said that before the 1973 Five Nations Championship, he was offered a £12,000 signing-on fee and at least £1,300 per season by Widnes Rugby League Club. He declined, but in September 1973 he succumbed to a similar approach from Warrington. In his first game against Castleford later that month, he charged over the line from some 20 metres out in typical Bevan fashion – with three defenders on his back – to score his first of over 200 tries for 'The Wire'. During his first season there the club won four trophies and in the following years J C played in eight other finals during his rugby league career, which lasted from 1973 to 1986.

He also won 17 caps for the Wales rugby league side and represented Great Britain in Test matches on four occasions. As a member of the Great Britain squad to tour

Australia and New Zealand in 1975, he scored 15 tries in 17 games, including three tries in the Test series against the Kiwis, reminding them of the devastating finishing powers he had displayed four years earlier with the British Lions. The fact that he also played flanker for Warrington and in the second row for Wales is further testimony of his unique combination of strength and mobility. Similarly his regular selection at centre, and as stand-off on one occasion for Wales, attested to rugby talents which often went unnoticed during his enthralling and thundering runs for the line.

Those particular talents were once again utilised to the benefit of rugby union in Wales when J C became Director of Coaching for the WRU. In that capacity he was coach of the Wales team at the under-19 World Cup in 1999, but he relinquished those duties the following year in order to take up an appointment at Monmouth School, as a teacher of Religious Education and Director of Rugby Coaching, a position which he still holds.

During his playing career he earned the nicknames of 'The Ox' and 'The Tylorstown Terror', both of which make reference to his forceful, aggressive running and his swashbuckling style. Neither does justice to the delight he took in his particular accomplishments. This however was frequently manifested in the fact that he loved to play the game with a smile on his face.

MERVYN DAVIES

U NLIKE SO MANY of his contemporaries in the Welsh team of the 1970s, 'Merv The Swerve' (apparently so named because of his surfboarding skills in Swansea Bay) had no pedigree of note as a rugby player, apart perhaps from being the son of a former Wales forward. He had played rugby as a three-quarter at Penylan Comprehensive School and was subsequently the star player in the Swansea Training College XV. There, his considerable height of 6'4" gave him certain advantages in the pack. In addition, his talents as a basketball player, which earned him selection for the Welsh Colleges basketball team, nurtured handling skills which stood him in good stead as a member of the back row. However his thin, gangly, rake-like appearance did nothing to suggest that in due course, he would become one of the greatest and most durable Number 8s in the world. It is said that one of the measures he took to try and belie the 'wimpish' appearance that he presented in the early days, was to grow a Mexican moustache!

While at college he was selected on one occasion by the All Whites, but made little impression and the club made no effort to retain his services. He moved to Surrey in 1969, to pursue a career as a teacher and turned out for the Old Guilfordians rugby team. After a few games he joined the London Welsh club and initially played for their third XV. Within a matter of months, he was selected for the first XV and took his place apprehensively (by his own admission) in the back row alongside Tony Gray and John Taylor.

A more phenomenal advance was to follow and, after only 6 games for London Welsh, he was selected for the Probables team in the final Welsh trial. Two weeks later he made an impressive debut for the Welsh team that defeated Scotland 17–3 at Murrayfield. That was the first of 38 consecutive caps for Mervyn Davies, a number which would have been considerably greater had he not been struck down by a tragic injury, at the age of 29 years, when playing for Swansea at a time when he had become the world's most capped Number 8.

Prior to that incident, he had captained Wales to eight victories in nine matches, a run which had started with a remarkable victory, by 25–10, against France in Paris, when six players had worn the red shirt for the first time. His last match for Wales was against France in Cardiff on 6 March 1976, when he captained the home side as they secured the Grand Slam with an exciting victory by 19–13. He had an inspired game despite having been steamrollered by the French pack in the opening minutes, with the ball nowhere near! One of the numerous studs that trampled him left a huge hole in his shin which would, in the case of some players, have ensured that they would not have been able to carry on. By the end of the game, the pain was excruciating. "There was a lot of internal bleeding going on: but it was important to the team to stay on. I dared not leave the field because we would have had only 14 men until a replacement arrived and that might have been time enough for France to score." That story epitomised the 'do or die' attitude which Mervyn possessed both as a player and as a captain who led by example.

'The incomparable Mervyn Davies', as described by J P R Williams, also played in eight tests for the British Lions, being on the losing side on just one occasion. At the time of his crucial injury in 1976, he had been unofficially asked by John Dawes, who had been selected as coach of the 1977 Lions for their tour of New Zealand, to captain the team, an invitation which Mervyn later admitted he would have proudly accepted, as it would have been his greatest honour in an illustrious career. There was universal agreement at the time that he would have been the ideal skipper. He retired having been a crucial part of a Wales team that won two Grand Slams, three Triple Crowns and four outright Championships during his career.

His attributes as a player were innumerable. Firstly, his defensive qualities were immense and manifested a durability and strength of character which far exceeded the usual demands on a Number 8. A former Wales coach stated that he had never seen anybody fall as bravely and so frequently on the ball as Mervyn Davies, which normally occurred in the face of flying boots that were intent on causing physical damage. In that connection, he was an expert at tidying up loose ball behind his forwards.

When asked what facet of the game gave him most satisfaction, he replied that tackling was his greatest pleasure. He was an expert at flattening midfield runners, in skilfully turning the opposition in the tackle and also in stealing the ball from opponents' hands in ensuing malls. In his opinion he probably made 40 tackles for Wales which otherwise would have resulted in tries. In tandem with his devastating tackling in midfield was an ability to read the game intuitively and to close down potentially threatening spaces. His fellow team members in the first Test played by the Lions against South Africa in 1977 recall an early crunching tackle he made on Morne du Plessis, the celebrated Springbok Number 8. As a result of the sheer power of Mervyn's tackle, the South African was knocked some yards backwards, bringing a gasp of disbelief from the partisan home supporters. They had probably never seen a 'Bok's forward being tackled so hard in a Test match. The incident was considered as being crucial in setting the tone for the steel required by the Lions to ensure an invincible series.

Mervyn's contribution to the line-out was priceless. At his own team's throw-in, he would guarantee possession at the back and could also be depended upon to regularly disrupt the opposition throw. One of the advantages of his dominance in that aspect of the game was that Wales, for many years, were able to play two other players, namely John Taylor and Dai Morris, in their back row who were slightly shorter than average but who, due to other qualities, were able to forge an amazingly successful partnership with their Number 8.

Mervyn's attitude to the attributes required of an international rugby forward were significantly influenced by the Wales tour to New Zealand in 1969. The visitors were soundly beaten in two Test matches, during which the Welsh pack was completely overcome by the physicality of the All Blacks forwards. As a result, Mervyn came home determined to improve his upper body strength and the general standard of his play. When he returned there in 1971, it was obvious that he had succeeded in doing so.

His play during the series was inspirational. The Lions' captain, John Dawes, named Mervyn as the second most important Lion of the Test series, after Barry John. The visitors won by 2–1, with the last Test being drawn. Indeed the All Blacks legend, Colin Meads, was so impressed with his performance at the back of the line-out (where he outplayed the celebrated Ian Kirkpatrick and denied the home team such vital possession), and in open play, that he named him and Mike Gibson, the Irish centre, as the two players who had contributed most to the All Blacks' defeat.

Yet it is widely believed that he played his best rugby during the Lions tour to South Africa in 1974. His defensive performance during the four-match Test series was particularly effective. His dominance in the back row was such that the Springbok selectors, for these matches, resorted to using four different Number 8s in order to try and stifle his influence, albeit without success. Mervyn's achievements were all the more commendable since it was commonly believed at the start of the tour that he would be playing second fiddle to the English star, the late Andy Ripley.

Recognised as one of the fittest back row players of his era, he also displayed throughout his career seemingly inexhaustible stamina and remarkable resilience against sometimes fierce opposition. Coupled with an obdurate determination to never allow his spirit to weaken, he always gave one hundred percent. The manner in which his career came to an end was therefore all the more poignant.

During a Welsh Cup semi-final match against Pontypool at the Cardiff Rugby Club ground on Sunday, 26 March 1976, when running in support of his three-quarters in open play, Mervyn suddenly collapsed to the ground from a brain haemorrhage. He almost died on the spot, but was able to draw upon the excellent medical facilities available at the stadium and the specialised care offered at the neurological unit of the University of Wales Hospital, where he underwent major surgery and remained on the danger list for a week. He recovered well, but was left with defective co-ordination and a deterioration in eyesight and smell.

It appeared that the haemorrhage was the second that Mervyn had suffered. Following a match between London Welsh and London Irish on 1 April 1972, he collapsed in the shower. He was taken to a local hospital which did not specialise in neurological matters and where he was diagnosed with meningitis, namely inflammation of the membrane enclosing the brain. In retrospect, it is believed that if brain tests had been undertaken following that first incident, they would have established that there was a weakness in the nerve ends of the brain which manifested itself during the fateful match at Cardiff. If that had been the case, it is more than likely that Mervyn would have had to retire from the game in 1972.

The world of rugby was stunned by the tragedy in 1976, at a time when Mervyn was playing at the peak of his game and had established himself as probably one of the best Number 8s ever. In 2002, in a poll of the rugby-going public by the Welsh press, on the occasion of the inauguration of the Welsh Rugby Former International Players Association, Mervyn Davies was voted the greatest ever Wales Number 8 and also the greatest ever Welsh captain.

GARETH EDWARDS

THE MOST SUCCESSFUL Welsh rugby team ever, which dominated the Five Nations Championship during the 1970s, was able to draw upon the talents of some of the best rugby players the world has ever seen, none less so than Gareth Edwards. Since his retirement in 1978, there have been countless polls of fans, critics and celebrated players to determine who was either the greatest Welsh ruby player ever, or the greatest in the history of world rugby. The winner has invariably been Gareth Edwards. His superiority is encapsulated in the words of the legendary Cliff Morgan: "Of all the players I've known during 50-odd years' involvement with the game Edwards stood head and shoulders above the rest."

He won 53 caps for Wales, scoring 20 tries, and represented the British Lions in Test matches on ten occasions. Yet, perhaps one of his greatest achievements was that all his appearances in the red shirt were consecutive, in that he never missed a Wales game through injury, nor was he ever dropped from the team. That, in itself, is ample testimony not only to his immense talent, but to his remarkable fitness, durability and resilience, especially in the light of the total commitment and controlled aggression which were such essential aspects of his game. Indeed, during his eleven-year career at the top, he never once suffered a bad injury, never broke a bone and never had a wound that required stitches. The injuries that did sometimes come his way were muscular and usually healed fairly quickly.

Ironically, at the outset of his rugby career, as a pupil at Pontardawe Secondary Technical School, Gareth Edwards was deemed too small to play in his chosen position of centre. Upon the advice of his games teacher, Bill Samuel, who was to play a profoundly important role in his all-round development, Gareth opted for the scrum-half position. He soon won his first representative honour with Swansea Valley Schoolboys but at that stage, according to Bill, "he did not reveal any promise at all. He was just a small run-of-the-mill schoolboy scrum-half... Many of his contemporaries were infinitely better than he was because of their size, speed and strength. He had to build up a survival mechanism based on the acquisition of skill, speed and strength."

However the rigorous programme of circuit and weight training, which his teacher devised for the class, would serve him well on the rugby field, and he soon began to enhance his physical development. Under the perceptive eye of his sagacious mentor, he also began to display a variety of other skills. With dedication and determination he became an excellent gymnast and an accomplished athlete. In addition, during his time at the school, he attained an impressive list of achievements in disciplines which, in the opinion of Bill Samuel, would be allied to the requirements of a top-class rugby player. For example, he decided to turn Gareth into a hurdler because he believed that the running style demanded by that particular event was similar to that required by a scrum-half. In due course, he became the Welsh schools long jump and 220-yard hurdles champion and, on winning the Welsh Games Championship in the 110-yard hurdles, was voted the most promising athlete in Wales by the

Western Mail. He was also a very promising pole-vaulter and, if adequate coaching facilities had been available in the Swansea Valley area at that time, it was considered that he would have represented Britain in that event in due course.

For the final two years of his school education, Gareth won a scholarship to Millfield, the prestigious English public school. Despite the fact that rugby now became his main sporting activity, while studying there his athletic prowess blossomed further. He broke the English School Championship record for the low hurdles, beating the eventual British Olympian, Alan Pascoe. He represented England in the British Championships, during which he lined up alongside two future rugby colleagues, Alan Martin and JJ Williams, who were representing the Welsh Schools team.

Yet there was another sport at which he excelled,

to such an extent that the manager of Swansea Town Football Club, Trevor Morris, travelled to his home village of Gwauncaegurwen to acquire his signature. Gareth had been making a name for himself as a youth player with Colbren Rovers and had appeared in a final trial for the Wales youth team. He also turned out for the Swansea Town youth team, scoring two goals for them in the final of the Welsh Youth Cup. Playing alongside him at Swansea, for example, was Georgio Chinaglia, who went on to represent Italy in the 1974 World Cup, and who eventually became President of Lazio Football Club. Gareth, at that point, was actively considering the possibility of forging a career in professional football, but his eventual acceptance by Millfield led him in other directions.

Having reaped the benefit of astute coaching from Bill Samuel, much of which had been on a one-to-one basis, Gareth adapted well to the rugby-orientated environment of Millfield, and his game got better and better. He had already played for Glamorgan against Munster at full-back before leaving Pontardawe Tech and now, although boarding at an English school, he was selected to represent the Welsh Secondary Schools under-19 rugby team. In due course he became a student at Cardiff College of Education with the intention of becoming a teacher. Although he was required to represent the college rugby team, mainly in midweek games, Bill Samuel, on whom Gareth still depended for advice, had already made some enquiries as to whether certain first-class rugby clubs would like to sign him. It appeared that Swansea Rugby Club weren't interested, but Cardiff Rugby Club invited him to their trials in September 1966. He soon played himself into the first team, for whom, over a period of twelve seasons, he appeared on 195 occasions, scoring 67 tries.

Within two months he was selected for the Welsh trials and made his first appearance for Wales against France in April 1967, playing inside David Watkins, who was also his half-back partner for the following match. For his third game for the national side, against the All Blacks at the Arms Park, Gareth played alongside Barry John, forming one of the most celebrated half-back pairings that ever represented Cardiff, Wales and the British Lions. They played together in the Welsh team on 23 occasions, until the retirement of the mercurial outside half from Cefneithin. On the occasion of his fifth cap Gareth, at the age of twenty years and seven months, was selected captain of the team, the youngest ever Wales player to be bestowed with that honour at the time. He performed that duty on 13 occasions in all, but many were of the opinion that it was perhaps unfortunate that such an uninhibited and talented player should be somewhat shackled by the additional responsibilities of the captaincy at such a young age.

It is generally agreed that, as a player, Gareth possessed all the skills and attributes required of a top-class scrum-half, which he applied at the highest level. From that early age, under Bill Samuel's tutelage, he had developed speed, power and incredible upper body strength, which he continued to work on throughout his career. He was 5'8" tall and in his prime weighed 12 stone 5 lbs which, coupled with the incredible force generated by his body, enabled him to shake off so many would-be tacklers. From close to the try line he appeared unstoppable as he blasted his way through all forms of attempted defence with breathtaking powers of acceleration. On such occasions, in the words of the authors of *Fields of Praise*, "the coiled inner spring he unwound whiplashed its way to triumph upon glorious triumph". He was a constant forager and his penetrative bursts frequently created space for his half-back partner or other colleagues who happened to be in support. His strength was complemented by a particularly low centre of gravity and a unique sense of balance, which no doubt had been honed by his earlier gymnastic training. He also used these talents to the utmost effect when subjecting opponents to many a crunching tackle. In addition, he was an accomplished kicker from the hand, an ability which often earned the appreciation of his forwards.

His passing skills were described by Barry John, who was renowned for his ability to create time and space for himself, as follows: "With Gareth's long pass, the best in the world, I had even more time… He had such terrific upper body strength that even when he was badly off balance he could still get the ball out to me. Some of the passes only travelled five yards but they would take ten players out of the game because nobody believed he could possibly get the ball out to me from such hopeless positions." This particular aspect of Gareth's superiority on the field was again nurtured by his dedication. For, in his early days, he would practice passing with a ball filled with sand in order to develop distance. In order to vary direction, he would also suspend a car tyre from a rope and endeavour to pass the ball through its centre as it swung to and fro.

Coupled with his more physical talents were some not so tangible traits which nonetheless made a significant contribution to his make-up as the complete player. He was unrelentingly competitive and had seemingly limitless stamina. He possessed dogged determination and a mental hardness which often gave him an aura of indestructibility. His vision on the pitch was comprehensive and he developed a tactical awareness which he shrewdly deployed to his own and his colleagues' advantage.

As perhaps befits the world's greatest player, he was the scorer of two tries which are regularly referred to as the best two tries ever. The first was scored at Cardiff against Scotland in February 1972, and is considered to be the best individual try of all time. Following a blind side break from a scrum deep in the Wales half, Gareth swerved to avoid a tackle by the covering Arneil, chipped over the head of full-back Arthur Smith, booted the ball on and after a dramatic race desperately dived to secure the crucial touch down in the Arms Park mud. It was a move which, over a distance of 85 yards, had epitomised so many of Gareth's great qualities as a player – power, skill, determination, speed, stamina and agility.

The second try was scored during the Barbarians game against the All Blacks at Cardiff in 1973, and was the culmination of glorious teamwork. Phil Bennet, in response to Carwyn James's pre-match exhortation of, "Phil don't waste any time. Soon as you like, Take them on!" started a breathtaking handling movement with a series of scintillating sidesteps. Superb handling saw five other pairs of hands take play deep into the New Zealand half, at which point Gareth Edwards exploded into action and crashed over the line for a memorable score.

As a director of Cardiff Blues and a regular media pundit, Gareth still maintains an active interest in the game. During his retirement he has had more time to enjoy his other great passion, which is angling, and even in pursuit of such a comparatively docile pastime, he could still create a stir. For example in 1990, while fishing in Llandegfedd, he set a British angling record, which stood for two years, when he caught a pike weighing 45lbs 6oz!

CHARLIE FAULKNER

ONE OF THE biggest mysteries in Welsh rugby during the 1970s was the actual age of one Anthony George Faulkner, the Pontypool and Wales loose-head prop. When he was capped for the first time against France in 1975, he was, according to various sources, somewhere between 27 and 30 years old. He seemed to have been selected 'out of the blue' as it were, for the reputation of the Pontypool front row hadn't yet been established as the ultimate force it was to become. 'Charlie' had joined the club from Cross Keys, along with Bobby Windsor, for the 1972–3 season and helped to transform Pontypool from being the worst first-class side in Wales to being in due course the country's best team. Both had initially played together for Whiteheads, the team that represented the steelworks which gave them employment, and later, for Newport Saracens.

In fact Charlie was born on 1 February 1941 and was 34 years old when he played for Wales in Paris that first time. When he won the last of his 19 caps in 1979, he was 38 years old, having been on the losing side for Wales in the Five Nations Championships on only two occasions. It was generally thought that his reticence to confirm his actual age stemmed from his desire to keep the truth from the Welsh selectors lest they decided, after a while, that he was perhaps too old after all to represent his country. That explanation, however, seems unlikely in the light of the fact that Charlie played for Wales in two international matches in Japan in September 1975 and would consequently have been required to submit his passport to the WRU in advance of such a trip! However earlier that season he was seemingly acknowledged as being 29 years old!

When he joined Pontypool he was a fairly raw exponent of front row play. However, under the influence and inspiration of the coach, Ray Prosser, he became one of the most respected scrummaging loose-head props in the game. As a steelworker Charlie relied on his physical prowess to undertake his daily duties satisfactorily. He was also a Welsh judo international and held a black belt in that discipline (not that he openly resorted to any aspects of the particular sport on the rugby field!) and these factors doubtless helped him to perform his front row duties with distinction. Yet amongst his main attributes as a prop was a particular mental and physical hardness which sustained him at the highest level in one of the most competitive areas of the game.

Both with Pontypool and Wales, Charlie regularly set about grinding down his opposite number in the scrum. It was of paramount importance to him to gain superiority, both physically and mentally, in that area of the game. It was in the scrum that his strength, stamina and resolve were tested most severely. In Charlie's opinion, if he wasn't able to get the better of his opposite number in the tight it would have detrimental effect on his own performance in every other aspect of play. Similarly by gaining the upper hand in the scrum, the aim would be to get the opposing tight-head, and often the rest of his pack, to lose heart and the psychological battle. When the threat of Scottish front row superiority, where the two renowned props

Ray McLaughlan and Sandy Carmichael were formidable opponents, was once mentioned in a pre-match briefing for the Welsh team, Charlie famously responded with a remark which aptly illustrated his uncompromising approach. "We may go up, we may go down, but we're not going backwards!"

One of the best and strongest tight-head props ever was the Frenchman, Robert Paparemborde, whose particular anatomy made it difficult for his opposite number to get to grips with him in the scrum. According to Graham Price, Charlie was the only loose-head prop ever to cope comfortably with Paparemborde in the tight. "Charlie's solution lay in his own immense strength. He was able to force his head under the Frenchman and then bore into the most vulnerable area in the upper body, the side of the ribcage near the floating ribs... At his peak Charlie was the most ruthless loose-head scrummager I have ever played with or against."

In retirement Charlie, like Price, decried the changes in scrummaging laws which removed some of the physical challenges from that aspect of play. For example he believed that introducing the law that stated that the shoulders of the front row players, when engaging in the scrum, must not be lower than the hips weakened the contest. Indeed he was of the opinion that some law changes, for example, in the line-out, turned rugby into a 'sissies game'! Yet he recognised that, since the 'law of the jungle' often prevailed in the scrum when he was a player, it was just as well, from the safety aspect in particular, that referees now had greater control over that facet of the game.

Despite his emphasis on physical prowess, Charlie was no slouch in the loose. He conscientiously endeavoured to keep fit throughout his career and even went to greater lengths than those required at formal training sessions to ensure that his fitness levels were acceptable. It was argued that, because he was quite a bit older than most of his fellow players, he needed to make a little more effort to ensure that he was able to compete at the highest level. Despite the physically demanding nature of his job at the local steelworks in Newport, where toiling for hours in front of a hot furnace must have taken its toll, he would still spend his lunch times doing circuit training, usually in the company of Bobby Windsor, in the local park. Charlie was also often known to undertake personal training sessions during the evening before important international games. Although not renowned for his speed about the field, proof of his fitness was perhaps the fact that he was often seen in support of try scoring movements. Indeed, during his first season in the red jersey of Wales he crossed for a try against Ireland, much to his delight, and joined his two fellow members of the Pontypool trinity who had, in previous matches, appeared on the list of Welsh try scorers.

Charlie always considered it a great honour to play for his country, even though that often meant financial sacrifice. For he, like Bobby Windsor, did not get paid for the days they were on international duties. Indeed they were often out of pocket as a result, for on such occasions they would often lose the opportunity to work double shifts at the steelworks. Yet for Charlie there was compensation in being part of remarkably successful Welsh team that won two Grand Slams and four Triple Crowns. He was also a member of the first 'club' front row ever to play for the British Lions in 1977, against the Bay of Plenty, when he was flown out as a replacement on their New Zealand tour. When his playing days were over, he successfully pursued a coaching career, for example with Newport and the Wales under-21 team.

Many humorous quips were attributed to Charlie during his career and he was frequently portrayed as a loveable rogue. There is a tale, for example, told by Bobby Windsor, about both of them, along with a friend called Paddy, having to appear before Newport Magistrates Court. The three had been employed as bouncers at a Newport nightclub and, on the occasion of Bobby's selection for the British Lions tour, it was decided to hold a party in his honour at the club. At about five o'clock in the morning, Paddy drove them all home and when he got to Charlie's house, he clipped the rear of a parked car. They thought no more of it, but a witness to the incident informed the police and they were ordered to appear in court. The three made sure that their stories corresponded, namely that a cat had dashed into the road, forcing Paddy to swerve, whereupon he clipped the car in question. Whilst fully intending to return at some time to inform the owner of the parked car, they considered that it had been too early in the morning to do so at the scene. When Paddy was asked during his evidence to state the colour of the cat that had run out before them he replied "Black". When Charlie was later asked the same question he replied "Grey". The solicitor undertaking the cross-examination drew his attention to the fact that Paddy had said the cat was black, while Charlie had said it was grey, and asked him to explain the discrepancy. Charlie stood there poker-faced and said, "It was a frosty morning, sir". Everybody in the court room apparently had great difficulty in keeping a straight face, and all three were found not guilty!

SCOTT GIBBS

For most rugby enthusiasts the abiding memories of Scott Gibbs's exceptional career as an inside centre are encapsulated in two vastly contrasting incidents. The first was in 1997 when, as a British Lion, he displayed immense strength in flooring the huge Springbok prop, Os du Randt, who was called 'The Ox', in the second Test in Durban. The second was in 1999, as he danced past the despairing hands of would-be tacklers in the English defence to set up a last-gasp victory for Wales at Wembley. This latter accomplishment was a reminder that Gibbs also possessed the finer skills required of a top class attacking centre – speed on the burst, vision, an eye for the gap, a safe pair of hands and a devastating sidestep. Yet he is mainly remembered for the power of his ferocious tackling in defence, which led to Jonah Lomu describing him as the best tackler in world rugby, and his blockbusting runs in attack, which caused Jeremy Guscott to refer to him as the world's fastest prop! In many ways he was similar to Dr Jack Mathews, particularly with regard to his tackling. In that respect, he possessed the lethal ability to hit his opponent at speed and with explosive power, usually targeting a vulnerable area of the body just above the waist.

His skills as a tackler were honed as a young lad playing rugby at Ysgol Gyfun Llanharri and with the Pencoed youth team. In those days he was quite small for his age and, as a result, was unable to take opponents on physically.

He had to rely instead on his sidestep or on his speed to get the better of them. Yet, because he was usually the smallest member of his side, the opposition would target him when they were going forward, with the result that he was forced to work on his tackling to ensure that he kept his place in the team. Despite the physical demands involved, putting opponents on the floor was an aspect of the game that gave him particular pleasure. However, at an early age, he recognised that he needed to have a greater physical presence on the field, so he regularly attended a local gym run by an ex-power lifting champion for instruction in weight training.

His rise through the rugby ranks was rapid. In 1988 he won his first cap for the Wales Youth team and became its captain. Neil Jenkins was also in that team and ironically they were the only two members who proceeded to play rugby at first-class level. Gibbs was called upon to play a few games for Bridgend at senior level but because he wasn't able to claim a regular place in that team, he moved to Neath for the 1990–1 season. He soon made an impression and, after just ten games, was selected for Wales B against Holland. After a further five games with the Gnoll club, he was selected, at the age of nineteen, to play for Wales against England at the Arms Park, where he was in direct opposition to the formidable England centre partnership of Guscott and Carling. At the end of that season, Wales held the wooden spoon, having failed to win a single game, yet Gibbs not only kept his place in the team throughout but was voted Welsh Player of the Year for 1990–1, the youngest ever recipient of that award.

He left school at the age of sixteen to work in a local double-glazing workshop but, despite being very happy there, he had by this time decided to accept a position with a Cardiff independent television company. This gave him greater flexibility to take on the numerous demands from the media and other bodies which were being generated by his new-found fame. Yet, he now entered upon an unsettling period in his career. He was approached by Wigan Rugby League Club as to the possibility of his moving to play there. He went on tour to Australia with Wales, where some storming performances led to his being called 'the pocket battleship'. Yet the tour was a disappointment in many respects as was his involvement in the 1991 World Cup, by the end of which Gibbs had played in only one victorious Welsh team during a twelve month period.

In January 1992 he joined Swansea, where Mike

Ruddock was coach and where he hoped he would see more of the ball than had been the case at Neath. Yet despite his apparent satisfaction with his lot at Swansea, he continued to be a target for rugby league clubs, with Hull and Wigan making determined efforts to sign him. His reputation was further enhanced as a member of the British Lions party to tour New Zealand in 1993, where his performances were so impressive as to oust Will Carling from the inside centre position for the second and third Tests. On his return St Helens Rugby League Club approached him with a substantial offer which was deflected by the efforts of Swansea and the WRU to retain his services. Nevertheless, despite having suffered a serious injury when playing for the Barbarians against the All Blacks in December 1993, and despite further enticements by Swansea, he signed for St Helens in April 1994. However this resulted in considerable acrimony between Gibbs and the Swansea club.

He readily adapted to the style of league rugby and his particular attributes as a player ensured that he became a great success. He loved the degree of physical confrontation that is such an inherent part of that game, but which was not so prevalent in rugby union. "Everything hurts after a game of rugby league: your ears, your eyebrows, your whole body. I could hardly walk up the stairs for days following a match… I couldn't get enough of it." He tasted considerable success with St Helens, such as winning the Rugby League Challenge Cup and the Super League Championship. He played for the Welsh Rugby League Team and enjoyed representing his country in the World Cup in 1995. Yet on 26 July 1996, he played his last game of Rugby League. In the newly arrived professional era rugby union clubs were now offering players attractive financial terms and Gibbs, having been approached by several English clubs, opted to return to Swansea Rugby Club.

By his own admission his experience of rugby league had made him a better player. Its demands had led to his making specific provisions in the gym to develop greater power and physique. He now weighed almost three stones heavier than when he started his rugby union career, and his chest and neck measurements had increased considerably. Upon his return to rugby union he employed his physicality to even greater effect than he'd done prior to going north. This was amply illustrated during the Lions tour to South Africa in 1997. The Springboks traditionally take great pride in physically intimidating and dominating their opponents and they attempted to do so in that series. However, inspired in particular by the stoic efforts of Scott Gibbs, the Lions won the series by two tests to one.

From the outset Gibbs literally left his mark in South Africa with many telling hits. Against Natal he dramatically floored Ollie le Roux, called 'the Elephant Man', with a shuddering tackle which left the 20-stone prop in a daze. Similarly in the first test, he flattened Andre Snyman, the 'Boks winger, and then Andre Venter, which left the extremely well-built flanker needing treatment. Then, in the second test, there was the famous incident, which is mentioned above, when Gibbs, with ball in hand, ran through the 19-stone du Randt. "I hit him full on and must have caught him in a soft spot because he just collapsed on the deck and started moaning. I didn't feel a thing, but it obviously hurt him!" Gibbs was named 'Man of the Series' by sports writers in South Africa at the time and later that year was voted Welsh Sports Personality of the Year.

He also won the Man of the Match award following the last of his 53 games for Wales in 2001, having scored two tries in the victory against Italy. He travelled to Australia with the British Lions later that year but did not appear in any of the Test matches there. He captained Swansea for five successive seasons from 1998–9 to 2002–3 and played for the club until his retirement in 2004. It would seem, in the light of his particular talents, that he would have been ideally suited to the modern game. This opinion is echoed by Stephen Jones, the *Sunday Times* rugby correspondent, who appropriately described Scott Gibbs as "the prototype of the twenty-first century rugby player".

RAY GRAVELL

During Ray Gravell's tenure in the Wales team between 1975 and 1982, a banner often seen on the terraces read 'Ray Gravell Eats Soft Centres'. It was a subtle play on words to indicate the supporters' appreciation of his hard, uncompromising style which was in evidence during his 23 appearances in the Welsh jersey. Apart from the rugged, swashbuckling appearance afforded by his strong, sturdy build and his reddish beard, his powerful and destructive forays in midfield often left prostrate opponents in their wake. He was just as aggressive in the tackle and firmly believed in imposing his physical presence on the opposition as soon as possible during a game. His mantra in that connection became one of the most notable of rugby quotations… "Get your first tackle in early, even if it's late"!

He became known as a master of the crash-ball technique whereby, having received the ball in full flight, he would blast his way through attempted tackles with forceful, direct running complemented by a ferocious hand-off and powerful acceleration. Yet, he possessed many other more subtle attributes which contributed to his reputation as a formidable centre. His attacking thrusts weren't always confined to scattering would-be defenders but were at times undertaken to create space on which his wingers could capitalise, which they did on so many occasions. He was also a sensitive handler of the ball and possessed excellent passing skills which had been honed at

the one-to-one sessions he had received during his early days at Llanelli Rugby Club from his mentor and coach, Carwyn James.

Despite his physical approach to the game he was never considered to be a dirty player. Yet, when the occasion demanded illicit retribution, he was prepared to respond in kind. For example, during Wales's first Test match on their tour of Australia in 1978, Grav was punched so hard in the face by his opposite number, Martin Knight, as they crossed to take up positions for the kick-off, that he fell to his knees and took some time to recover. At that point he considered that he had two choices. He could either dismiss the incident, thus giving his opponent a psychological advantage before the game had even begun, or, respond in robust fashion. He chose the latter option and when Knight, during the opening minutes of the game, earnestly pursued a high kick from Paul Maclean, his outside half, Grav confessed to ignoring the ball and concentrating on ensuring that Knight wouldn't be getting to his feet for a while!

In complete contrast to his fearless commitment and macho image on the field of play, Grav, throughout his career as a rugby player, constantly sought reassurance from his peers that his performance was acceptable and in that respect displayed an insecurity which was sometimes the cause of consternation amongst his colleagues. At three o'clock, on the morning of his first game for Wales in Paris in 1975, his room-mate, JJ Williams, awoke to find that Grav had packed his bag and was all set to go home. He was apparently overcome by the occasion and couldn't face the pressures ahead, until JJ managed to persuade him that all would be well. Much to the concern of many colleagues who shared a room with him on rugby journeys, he was a notoriously bad sleeper and, while touring with the British Lions in South Africa, he woke Jeff Squire early one morning to ask "Jeff, did I sleep all right?" On that particular tour he was the only Lions three-quarter to have appeared in all four tests against the Springboks, which in itself was testimony to his skill and physical competence in such a demanding environment.

He was also, by his own admission, a chronic hypochondriac who was often convinced that the slightest ailment could be the precursor of some dreadful illness which would end his career. He was sometimes prepared to accept a lesser fate, as on the occasion when JJ was shaken awake by a sniffing Grav at 6.00 a.m. on the morning of a game, to be asked whether he thought Grav had bronchitis! However when on duty with Llanelli, Grav could draw comfort from the services of Bert Peel, the club sponge man and masseur, for whom he had the greatest respect and affection. Whenever he complained of an injury or a health problem, Bert often acted more in the capacity of a psychologist and social worker than as a practitioner of medical cures. For example, it took Grav years to realise that, on the occasions he had complained to Bert that he was suffering from a headache, and was consequently reassured by pills which seemed to have the desired effect of restoring him to perfect health, he had the whole time been swallowing Smarties, which had been especially doctored by the trainer! During one game Grav, having received a blow to his leg, called for attention from Bert, who performed the customary massage. He was then pronounced fit enough to resume and had been playing for some minutes, with no apparent discomfort, before realising that Bert had been massaging the leg that hadn't been injured!

His colleagues at club and international level would agree that it would be difficult to find someone who played the game with more passion than Grav. This was particularly true of the occasions when he wore the red jersey of Wales. According to Carwyn James, no-one wore that jersey with greater pride than Grav, who confessed that "nothing beats playing for your country. It is and always has been the privilege of the few, something to treasure for life. I have been very fortunate." His enthusiasm for his country, its language and culture was unbridled and primarily inspired by two factors. Firstly, by the discussions and conversations he had with Carwyn James, who was himself an ardent nationalist, during his early years at Stradey. Secondly, as a result of numerous visits to the Emerald Isle, by his acquaintance with the political and patriotic history of Ireland, which served to arouse his own awareness of the importance of Welsh nationhood.

Such feelings were manifested in the dressing room before every game when Grav would take great delight in singing in Welsh the songs of Dafydd Iwan, a particular hero of his. Grav claimed that the words of those songs always inspired him to greater things on the field and, although this practice could perhaps be slightly disturbing for his colleagues, they were prepared to accept that it gave him the necessary confidence to perform. For, in that dressing room before a game, Grav usually had a nervous, noisy and agitated presence which led to some of his colleagues complaining that he made them feel tired before the game had started!

Sometimes that excitable nature got the better of him outside the changing room. On the occasion of his first cap in 1975, when lining up in the tunnel to take the field at Parc de Princes, he was unable to stop himself from punching one of the French team who was standing beside him (a huge forward at that) hard on the shoulder. Early during another game against France, at the same location in 1981, he found himself at the bottom of a ruck, with his hands wrapped around the neck of the nearest Frenchman and shouting "Froggie! Froggie! Froggie!" When he realised it was the formidable flanker, Jean-Luc Joinel, he instantly released him, with the conciliatory comment "Only joking! Only joking!" Shortly afterwards, when Grav was in the process of getting to his feet following a tackle, he received a solid blow to the face which made his head spin and his knees buckle. While the trainer was attending to the subsequent bleeding, Joinel strolled up and, with a smile, said "Only joking! Only joking!"

Yet, there is no doubt that the emotion generated by Grav often had a positive effect on his colleagues. Gareth Edwards recalls standing next to him when the Welsh national anthem was sung before that game in 1975. Although Gareth, by then a seasoned international player, was acquainted with the passions which could be aroused by the singing of 'Hen Wlad Fy Nhadau', he confessed that he had never heard anyone sing the words with greater gusto and conviction than that expressed by Grav on that occasion and admitted that, as a result, he himself had never sung the anthem with such feeling. Grav's fervour for promoting the use of the Welsh language sometimes bore fruit in unexpected quarters. For example, he was delighted that his colleague in the Wales team, Bobby Windsor, a Gwent man through and through, had sent his two sons, Luke and Sean, to Bryn Onnen Primary School and Gwynllyw Secondary School, so that they could be educated through the medium of Welsh.

His regard for Llanelli Rugby Club was unparalleled. His links with Stradey began as a seventeen year old, when, following some stirring performances for the Queen Elisabeth Grammar School team, he was invited to play for Llanelli Youth, which led to his being selected to play for Wales at that level. Over the next fifteen years, he was to appear for the Scarlets on 485 occasions, scoring 120 tries. He was elected captain of Llanelli for the 1980–1 and 1981–2 seasons, which he deemed to be the second greatest honour of his playing career, only surpassed by the award of his first cap for Wales. Similarly, he was the youngest member of the Llanelli team that famously defeated the All

Blacks in 1972, another achievement which he rated very highly on his list of personal accomplishments. Following his retirement as a player, he became, in due course, a valued and respected President of the club. Phil Bennet aptly described his commitment to the Scarlets: "If there was some way of wiring him up to a generator then the electrical charge that seems to run through him when he talks about Llanelli could keep the whole town alight for days."

For many years prior to having to succumb to the devastating effects of diabetes, he had acted as ceremonial sword bearer for the Gorsedd of Bards at the National Eisteddfod, a duty which was an immense source of pride to him. He had, during that period, immersed himself in the history and functions of that important national institution and become a great admirer of all its activities, to the extent that he admitted, "If I could wish to be someone other than who I am, that wish, without any doubt, would be to be a bard, for I would be prepared to forfeit every cap that I have won with Wales and the British Lions if only I could have the thrill of getting to my feet, in the glare of the National Eisteddfod pavilion spotlight, as the bard who had won the Eisteddfod chair or crown."

His regard for his native village of Mynydd y Garreg, near Cydweli, was compelling. Wherever he travelled he always hankered after the comfort and security afforded by his family, his home and his locality. The decision many years ago to name a road in the village after him, Heol Ray Gravell, is one indication of the esteem and affection his community had for him. In 1976, following Llanelli's victory in a Welsh Cup semi-final match against Bridgend, he was offered £25,000 by Hull, made up of a £15,000 tax-free signing-on fee, plus £10,000 over two years, to play rugby league. In those days, especially in the light of his comparatively limited previous earnings as an electricity board linesman and later as a sales representative, the Hull offer was indeed lucrative. Yet Grav declined since he couldn't bear the thought of having to live outside Wales, and his community in west Wales in particular.

In 1985 he was offered a contract to work for the BBC with the result that he decided to forego his playing days with his beloved Llanelli. Following his retirement he enjoyed a successful career as a radio presenter of chat and entertainment shows and as a respected television pundit on rugby programmes on S4C, the Welsh-language television service. In that connection, his infectious enthusiasm and his warm, unassuming personality gained him countless fans and left a lasting impression on those who met him, from all walks of life. He also made his mark in the field of acting and appeared in a number of films, with stars such as Jeremy Irons and Peter O'Toole. On one occasion, when O'Toole was receiving make-up on the first day of Grav's appearance on the set of *Rebecca's Daughters*, the make-up artist happened to mention that the person sitting at the far end of the trailer was an ex-rugby player. O'Toole, a great rugby fan, soon realised who the Welshman was, whereupon he shouted in delight, "Well, f★★★★★★ hell. You wait until I get back to London and tell them that I'm making a film with Ray Gravell!" From that point on, O'Toole was constantly at Grav's side on set, and whenever he was asked to have obligatory promotional photographs taken, he would refuse unless Grav was included in the shot!

After battling bravely for some years against the effects of the most serious form of diabetes, Grav died on 31 October 2007, from a heart attack while on holiday with his family in Spain. Ironically, it occurred exactly 35 years to the day of one of the highlights of Grav's career, which was the celebrated Llanelli victory against the All Blacks. During his funeral service at Stradey Park, the club scoreboard poignantly carried the result, Llanelli 9 Seland Newydd 3. The occasion was reminiscent of a state funeral, with ten thousand mourners in attendance and the First Minister, Rhodri Morgan, amongst those who gave an address. It was indeed a fitting tribute to a proud Welshman and a giant of the rugby field. In the world of rugby and subsequently in the field of broadcasting, no person was held in greater esteem and whenever people spent time in Grav's company, he always left them feeling better about themselves and about life in general.

TERRY HOLMES

O N 31 AUGUST 1986, Terry Holmes, after a very distinguished ten year career with Cardiff Rugby Union Club, made his home debut for Bradford Northern at the Odsall Stadium. Following that game Jim Mills, who had played rugby union for Cardiff before becoming one of the star forwards of the league game in the 1960s, remarked that, in his opinion, Holmes was not a rugby league scrum-half. On the other hand, he believed that he would be turned into an accomplished loose forward by Bradford Northern. That comment reflected a frequently held opinion in union circles that one of Holmes's attributes during his playing career with Cardiff and Wales was his ability to operate as a ninth forward.

He himself considered this to be unflattering and inaccurate, in that, as a scrum-half of above average build (he was six feet tall and weighed thirteen stone), he was simply able to use his strength and power as a natural part of his game. However, he had many other more sophisticated talents that made him one of the best scrum-halves in world rugby. He cultivated a long, accurate pass which gave his partner at outside-half ample time and space in which to operate effectively. He could read a game instinctively and intelligently, and his acute awareness of lapses and deficiencies in opposition defences enabled him to exploit such weaknesses decisively. He would accomplish this with devastating solo runs or by committing defenders in such a way as to create space for his colleagues.

Yet, by his own admission, he thoroughly enjoyed the physical contact upon which his game thrived, and he became conditioned to physical confrontation. One of his basic duties, as he saw it, was to take out opponents on the fringes of set pieces and loose play, working in close conjunction with his back row. His was literally a game of hard knocks from which he derived no little pleasure. Perhaps this is reflected in the fact that he relished, for example, the battles that regularly took place between Cardiff and Pontypool and which he described as being usually physical and rough but rarely dirty. He considered Ponty to be the most difficult Welsh side to beat, but a side which always brought out the best in him. This in itself, perhaps, is an indication of the extent to which Holmes thrived on hard, physical encounters.

As well as playing in almost 200 games for Cardiff and scoring over 100 tries, he made 25 appearances for Wales, during which he crossed for nine tries. The vast majority of those scores were accomplished in typical Terry Holmes fashion, whereby he would take on the opposition from within ten metres and blast his way to the line, making full use of his explosive power and his piston-like hand-off. His strength was an innate asset, but it was also nurtured by the nature of his daily work with a scrap company. His job was largely concerned with demolishing disused factories and warehouses and disposing of the metal acquired to firms which were involved in reprocessing. It was a dangerous and physically demanding occupation, which frequently required a good head for heights and a capacity to handle heavy objects. Weight training, in the present era, forms an essential part of the conditioning programmes at rugby clubs. Yet Holmes admitted

that, until he went to Bradford Northern, he hadn't appreciated the benefits of such a discipline. In addition to his normal training requirements there, he fitted his own garage with appropriate weight training equipment, which resulted in a marked improvement in his already renowned power.

Terry Holmes was born on 10 March 1957 in 74 Churchill Way, Cardiff which was almost within kicking range of the National Stadium. The house was demolished some ten years later and the family moved to the Fairwater district of the city. He is a Cardiffian through and through, and was raised to be a likeable, street-wise member of the Irish community there. Although both his parents were born in the city, the family was from Irish stock, and he was brought up in the traditions of the Catholic faith. As a lad he became an altar boy at St David's Cathedral in neighbouring Charles Street. He would spend much of his spare time in that vicinity, for he would regularly help out on his mother's fruit and vegetable stall just off Queen Street. Phyllis was the lynchpin of the family and was very supportive of her two daughters' achievements in higher education and, from the outset, of Terry's rugby career. His father, Dai, who had various jobs as a seaman or in the docks, had his own interests, none of which were rugby. Terry tells the amusing story, which illustrates Dai's indifference to the sport, of seeing his father on one particular occasion, riding past on his bike while wearing Terry's official Welsh team blazer. He was apparently completely unaware of its significance to his son!

Terry first represented Cardiff in the city's under-11 schools team and, following sound rugby grounding at Bishop Hannon RC High School, he joined Cardiff Youth at the age of sixteen. He was soon selected for the Wales Youth team and remained a member for a lengthy three year period, winning a record number of caps. He made his first appearance for Cardiff against Newport in 1975, at the age of 17, the day after he had led the Cardiff and Districts Youth team to victory over Bridgend Youth. For his second match, against Pontypool, he was joined at outside half by Gareth Davies, who was making his first appearance for the club. This was the beginning of a famous and extremely successful half-back partnership that endured for almost the whole of their respective union careers.

It is commonly believed that Holmes was injury prone during both his union and league careers and it is a fact that he was out of action for significant periods as a result of his endeavours on the field. Yet, his first two serious injuries did not result from the demands of first-class rugby.

Firstly, at the age of 18 he broke his ankle when playing basketball for his local youth club and then, two years later, he suffered the same injury when playing rugby in a local fun match. He then had four trouble-free years before being sidelined for two weeks on the 1980 British Lions tour of South Africa with a dislocated shoulder. However, in his first game back, he suffered from torn ligaments and had to return home. Similarly, in the first Test between the Lions and New Zealand in Christchurch in 1983, he suffered a knee injury and once again had to return home, becoming the only player ever to have to leave two Lions tours because of injury.

In November 1985 Terry Holmes joined Bradford Northern for a reputed £80,000, despite many reservations being aired in private and in public concerning his tendency to get injured for significant periods. Yet this was the fourth time that a rugby league club had tried to capture his signature – for his achievements and his reputation as a hard, courageous and uncompromising competitor made him a celebrated acquisition. In his first appearance for Bradford in December at Swinton, before a crowd of 5,700, which was three times greater than their average attendance, he dislocated his shoulder again early in the game. Being acutely aware of the expectations of the club and the spectators, he foolishly tried to fight his way through the resulting pain for some time before being forced to leave the field. In his next match, five weeks later, for Bradford A against Battley A, he fell on his elbow in a tackle and dislocated his shoulder again. Lesser men would probably have thrown in the towel at that stage but he underwent surgery during the spring of 1986 and fought his way back to fitness in readiness for the coming season, during which he gave many stirring performances.

However after a total of 40 appearances for Bradford Northern, he incurred another serious injury in October 1987, in the Yorkshire Cup final against Castleford. Consequently, the torn ligaments that he suffered in that match led to his regretfully announcing his retirement. Terry Holmes would argue that, in a game of such fierce physical contact, both in rugby union and rugby league, injuries are part and parcel of any player's career, and that he was not particularly prone to injury. In support of this claim, he states that he rarely suffered from those fairly minor injuries which seemed to plague so many other players and which would frequently lead to their missing a match or two every so often. In addition many of the serious injuries which he incurred were the result of bad luck. For example, the ligament trouble which forced him to return from the Lions tour to South Africa, was the result of an awkward landing after taking a short throw to the back of the line. His shoulder injury against Swinton was due to a freak accident when a half-hearted tackler grabbed his arm before twisting it sharply.

Nevertheless, the fact that he played the game with such ferocity and such disregard for his personal wellbeing must have placed him in greater danger than most. Yet there were few recriminations in the light of his apparent failure to fulfil the expectations of the Bradford rugby league enthusiasts. They appreciated the fact that he had bravely battled against serious injury problems without ever whingeing about his lot, and that he had always played with passion and total commitment in the Bradford colours, as indeed he had done with Cardiff, Wales and the British Lions. For many years after leaving Yorkshire, he undertook coaching duties with Cardiff and Caerphilly rugby clubs. In recent years he served for a time as coach to the Wales Deaf rugby union squad.

GARIN JENKINS

A MONG THE MANY achievements and personal records that befell Garin Jenkins as a player, it is more than likely that one of the accomplishments that gave him particular pleasure was the fact that he played for King Country in New Zealand, for a whole season, at the age of 21, as a tight-head prop. During this time he more than held his own against his Kiwi adversaries and on occasions came face to face with some of the best forwards in world rugby at the time. Despite playing in an unfamiliar position, and despite not having previously played a single first-class game in Wales, he impressed the King Country team manager, the great Colin Meads, to such an extent that he was informed by the 'Pine Tree', after his final game there, that if he ever wanted to return to play rugby in New Zealand, there would always be a place for him in the King Country team.

Forwards, particularly those in the front row, don't survive the rigours of top-class New Zealand rugby unless they possess a particular hardiness and a determination to impose themselves upon their opponents. Garin, for example, amply illustrated these attributes for King Country in a game against Auckland, the country's leading team at the time. Most of them were All Blacks and had contributed to their country's victory in the previous year's World Cup competition. As holders of the Ranfurly Shield, they were required to defend their position against three teams. They chose to play Wellington, Canterbury

and King Country. They gained overwhelming victories against the first two of these teams, but were made to fight all the way by Garin and his fellow players. The score of 28–0 to Auckland would seem to suggest a comfortable win, but this was far from being the case.

It was the general opinion at the time that the King Country pack had more than held their own in a particularly hard battle. The opposing props were Steve McDowell, who was already an All Black legend, and the giant Samoan, Peter Fatialofa. In the scrums Garin had been making life a little uncomfortable for Peter, so during an early line-out, the Samoan took a hefty swing at his Welsh opponent and broke his nose. According to Garin that was 'all part of the package' and he played on, without complaining, for the remainder of the game. His reward was a supply of free beer throughout the evening, provided by his new-found admirers, McDowell and Fatialofa!

Throughout his career he had always accepted that playing in the front row entailed being subjected to considerable physical provocation. Yet he seemed always to disregard any injustice he might have suffered in that respect. For example, during the 1999 World Cup when playing for Wales against Argentina he was the victim of one of the most blatant examples of eye-gouging ever seen in international rugby and a photograph of the incident became world famous. Garin gave evidence to the World Cup disciplinary panel investigation and did his best to play down the incident. He explained that he hadn't been aware of any deliberate attempt to gouge and suggested that the culprit seemed to have accidentally left his hand behind on his face following a scrum!

Garin was not a dirty player but, nevertheless, he gained a reputation as being rather impetuous and undisciplined at times and was banned from playing for specific periods on more than one occasion. He was also known as a plain speaker, one who was prepared to voice his opinion, as the occasion demanded, particularly in the light of an apparent injustice. There is a tale of how he stood up to Graham Henry when he had just started out as the Welsh coach in 1998. So that he could acquaint himself with the leading Welsh players prior to selecting his first squad to play South Africa, he arranged two trial matches involving 70 players. He then named his squad, which included a number of players who hadn't been involved in the trials, and which had one vacancy for the position of hooker. Since he had previously stated that he would be choosing his squad on the basis of what he had seen on the field, his announcement had riled Garin, who gave the ultimate 'Great Redeemer' a piece of his mind. It was thought at the time that his outburst would have put paid to his future chances as a Wales player but, to Garin's credit, and Henry's too, he eventually won over his coach and went on to win many more caps.

His penchant for plain speaking was further illustrated following the amazing, last-gasp Welsh victory, by 32–31, over England at Wembley in 1999. When asked, on live TV, immediately after the final whistle, for the reaction of the English front row Garin replied, "They had a few things to say at the start but by the end they were blowing through their arses!" He is affectionately known as a typical valleys 'character', always ready to tease his colleagues or regale them with a humorous quip, often at his own expense. When playing for Swansea against the Australians he decided he was, from the very first scrum, going to provoke his opposite number, Phil Kearns, possibly the leading hooker in the world at the time. So when the two front rows came together, Garin started with "I'm the Number One! I'm the Number One!" This continued for a number of scrums until Kearns eventually got fed up with Garin's antics and retorted with "Yeah! The number one shithead more like!" Apparently that was the first time those two packs had been in a scrum that had nearly collapsed because it was rocking so much with laughter.

When Garin left Wales to spend a year in New Zealand, he was a member of Ynys-y-bŵl rugby team and he returned to play for his native village following his stint overseas. He was now much tougher and harder, and obviously used to a standard of rugby which was greater than that provided by the lower divisions of Welsh league rugby. So he decided to try his luck with Pontypridd. Having played seven games for the first team as hooker, he realised that it was going to be very difficult to depose Phil John, the incumbent hooker there. Consequently, he responded to approaches from the Pontypool club and left Sardis Road early in 1989.

That was the beginning of what was to be an extremely profitable learning process for him. From the likes of Graham Price, Ray Prosser and John Perkins he obtained a firm "… grasp of the basic and fundamental principles involved. I was taught at Pontypool the intricacies of binding, pressure points, feet positions, stance and how to use the body to best effect in the scrum and how to pressurise opponents and exploit their weak points."

He soon established himself as one of the leading Welsh hookers and won his first cap against France in September 1991, prior to being chosen for the Welsh squad for the 1991 World Cup, where he appeared in all three pool games. He also played in the World Cup competitions of 1995 and 1999. On his return from the 1991 tournament, he joined the Swansea club and went on to gain 59 caps in all (thus overtaking the legendary Bryn Meredith), which is still a record for Welsh hookers. A lengthy career saw him establish himself as a hard, uncompromising and extremely able competitor, particularly in the set pieces. He was a match for some of the best hookers ever and was described by the celebrated Irish Number 2, Keith Wood, as his most respected opponent.

As a young boy Garin had a greater interest in soccer than rugby but due to the influence of his teacher, Dafydd

Idris Edwards, at Trerobert Primary School, he eventually began to enjoy playing rugby more. However at the age of 13 he began a particularly rebellious period in his life. Despite having loving and caring parents who, until that time, for example, had brought him up to go regularly to Sunday school, he went completely off the rails. He was expelled from Coedylan Comprehensive School, having refused to attend there for a period of nine months, and was sent away to home for 'naughty boys'. On his return, he attended Hawthorn School, Pontypridd until he left at the age of 15 years old.

He followed his father, and grandfather before him, to the local Lady Windsor Colliery where he stayed until he was made redundant at the age of 21. He was the last miner, in a distinguished line, to play for Wales. Although he hadn't worked on the coal face, his labouring job underground was manually demanding and subject to many of the dangers that had been responsible for 129 deaths at that particular colliery over a period of 100 years. Garin joined the Ynys-y-bŵl Youth rugby team after leaving school and attributes his involvement there as being his salvation from a life of rebellion and waywardness. Despite many instances of recklessness, his time there provided him with a discipline which he greatly appreciated.

He retired from playing in 2002 and is currently the elite youth development officer with the Ospreys Rugby Club. He has undertaken many overseas projects for the charity, Samaritan's Purse, and is a very popular speaker at sporting functions and at church gatherings. He is is a committed Christian and is of the opinion that if he'd held such beliefs during the early part of his career, he would have been a more successful player. He would have been inwardly stronger and would have had more discipline. He feels blessed that God has provided him with all the positive things in his life and that He has shown him so much grace over the years. "We can look back and think the best years are behind but living with Jesus the best is yet to come," he says.

DR JACK MATTHEWS

D R JACK MATTHEWS, born in 1920, is renowned as probably the hardest tackler in the history of Welsh rugby. He played centre three-quarter for Cardiff and appeared also in the colours of Bridgend and Newport. He was capped 17 times for Wales and represented the British Lions in six Test matches on their tour of Australia and New Zealand in 1950. Were it not for the interruption of the Second World War, his international rugby career would have been considerably more prolific. In the Cardiff and Wales jerseys, he formed a devastating centre partnership with the late Bleddyn Williams, his lifelong friend. Yet, often as a result of the erratic selection policies of the Big Five, they played alongside each other for their country on just five occasions.

Bleddyn would generously attribute much of his personal accomplishments to the selfless play of his co-centre. When reviewing their careers in an interview in the *Telegraph* some years ago he described Dr Jack's contribution to their success as follows:

> We used to run a lot of scissor moves – I always started with the ball and he would cut the angle. The first time I would feed Jack and he would get smashed. The second time I would feed him and he would get roughed up again. He would wink at me as he got up. "You know what to do now Bledd!" and the third time I would throw the dummy. He would get hit by two or three hard cases and I would

saunter off to score under the posts and get all the glory and headlines. But they were Jack's tries really!

Dr Jack first made a name for himself as a rugby player when he appeared for the Welsh secondary schools team, over a period of three years. In 1939 he played in the final Welsh trial while a sixth-former at Bridgend Grammar School and in 1940 he was chosen in the centre for Wales alongside Wilf Wooller in a game against England for which no caps were awarded. He had to wait until 1947 before he won that first cap, against the same opponents. During the next three years he was selected fairly regularly for Wales and played in every game for Wales in 1950, when they won the Triple Crown, and in 1951, when he captained his country for the first and only time in the last game of the championship against France. However, he was omitted from the team for the opening match of the following season against England at Twickenham.

Yet at midnight on the night before that game, he received a telephone call from the WRU asking him to travel to London early the following morning, as he would be playing for Wales in the afternoon instead of the injured Bleddyn Williams. He was met by the chairman of the Big Five, who confirmed that he would be one of the Welsh centres. So, Dr Jack proceeded to the dressing room to get changed. However, following a hastily convened meeting of the Big Five in the changing room toilets, he was told that he wouldn't be playing after all! He was naturally very annoyed and, having given the WRU officials a piece of his mind, he informed them that he never wished to be considered for selection for the Welsh team again. He continued to play for and captain Cardiff for the remainder

of the season but his international career had come to an
end on rather a sour note, which rankled considerably
with Dr Jack for many years.

Since his early days he had worked on the destructive element of his tackling. He continually nurtured his strength and power and, despite being just 5'8" tall, he used his 14 stones and 9 lbs to the utmost effect. As a young lad he would continuously practice, hurling himself forcibly at a heavy sandbag which he kept in the attic, in order to improve the power and timing of his tackling. Throughout his career he believed in accelerating into the tackle in order that he might knock bigger and heavier opponents backwards and, in later years, observed that tacklers in the modern era were generally lacking in that respect. In the interview in the *Telegraph* he described his philosophy when attempting to stop an opponent:

> Only one thing mattered, smashing him with a fair tackle the first time he ever received the ball. Nobody's immune from pain and suffering. Not even the legends. Hit them hard like that and they will be looking over their shoulders for the rest of the game.

His reputation as a deadly tackler had preceded him when he arrived in New Zealand as a member of the British Lions' touring party in 1950. However it was soon enhanced with a number of stirring performances as a result of which he was dubbed the 'Iron Man'. Doubtless the fact that he fractured the breastbone of the All Blacks' centre Ron Elvidge with a devastating tackle during the Test series, cemented his 'hard man' image. Fred Allen, who had just retired as a player with the All Blacks team and who became one of the most successful All Blacks coaches ever, described Dr Jack as 'the greatest head-on tackler I ever saw'. He analysed his technique with regard to that particular type of tackle as follows:

> The secret of his success at this most difficult of all the tackles was his surging acceleration into the victim's body. He went rather high, aiming about the stomach or the short ribs, and so avoided trouble with the runner's knees which are usually the daunting obstacle to front-on tackles. His acceleration deprived the ball-carrier of any chance to fend him off. It was thrilling to watch this technique so well displayed.

As a centre, his strength in the tackle was complemented with a blistering turn of speed. In 1937, he was the Welsh junior 220 yards champion, with a time of 24 seconds, and two years later he came second in the 100 yards senior championships. In addition, his powerful hand-off completed a very potent attacking force.

As well as being a well-respected Cardiff GP for over 50 years, Dr Jack also used his medical expertise in the service of sport. He was the medical officer for the British Lions in South Africa in 1980, and was a medical advisor to the Welsh regional council of the British Boxing Board of Control for many years. In that capacity he was on duty at many memorable title fights, involving such boxing stars as Tommy Farr, Henry Cooper and Joe Erskine. But perhaps he achieved his most notable success in the ring as a boxer. When he was a medical student in March 1943, he fought a draw, over three rounds, with an American GI stationed at St Athan. That soldier, called Rocky Marciano, embarked four years later on a professional boxing career that saw him retire as undefeated heavyweight boxing champion of the world, having won 43 of his 49 professional fights by knockout. Yet he had failed to put Dr Jack on the canvass!

At a press conference arranged by British Lions officials in Cardiff in 2004, in advance of their visit to New Zealand the following year, Dr Jack was very critical of the arrangements planned for the tour. He was rather scornful of the fact that Clive Woodward, the Lions coach (who had been one of the players under Dr Jack's medical care on the 1980 tour) intended to take 44 players to New Zealand for ten matches, along with 24 back-up staff. But his most scathing comment was reserved for the proposed appointment of a psychiatrist for the tour. Dr Jack informed the assembled gathering that "If players want to see a psychiatrist they shouldn't be playing rugby anyway!"

COURTNEY MEREDITH

C C MEREDITH, who played for Neath, Wales and the British Lions in the 1950s was the prop no one wanted to prop against. W O Williams, who, on the loose-head, propped with him in the Welsh jersey twelve times, remarked that he was glad that Courtney was on his side on those occasions, but that he could be a real problem for him in training, and in club matches, when they would often prop against each other. He confessed that "nobody gave me as much trouble as Courtney!" It was not uncommon to hear props physically creaking as a result of the tremendous pressure which C C exerted, which sometimes led to their changing sides in the scrum rather than allowing themselves to be subjected to further punishment from him.

What is remarkable is that he hadn't played prop until he joined Neath during the 1950–1 Season. He had spent the previous few years in the back row while representing Crynant in the West Wales League but, upon arriving at the Gnoll, he applied himself diligently to learning the art of propping. Although he suffered some early problems with his scrummaging, he soon mastered the techniques involved. To his immense credit he did this so successfully that he has been generally recognised as the finest prop of his era, who was, invariably, physically stronger than every prop who opposed him. By profession he was a production engineer with the Steel Company of Wales at the Abbey Works and, according to the rugby writer Huw

Richards, "he applied that expertise in stress, pressures and breaking points to formidable effect on the rugby field".

At 5'10" and weighing a little under 15 stone, he packed a tremendous amount of power into his scrummaging where he was, according to critics and colleagues alike, "solid as a rock". Second rows would regularly commend the tightness of his bind which consequently allowed them to exert so much more pressure on opposing packs in the scrum. At club level he displayed his versatility by playing sometimes at loose-head, instead of in his preferred tight-head position, a switch which few front row players can accomplish satisfactorily. He was fortunate in that he was part of a traditionally formidable Neath pack and when he was capped for the first time against Scotland in 1953, he was one of four Welsh all black forwards to be selected for Wales that season, and one of 14 Neath props to have appeared for their country during the post-war amateur era. It is said, however, that he had one significant drawback as a prop… he was far too good-looking!

He was a good jumper in short line-outs and was an excellent support player for ball winners such as Roy John and Rees Stephens, whom he played alongside in both the Neath and Wales teams. He displayed other traits which distinguished him from many others who played in his position, in particular considerable mobility around the field. This attribute doubtless stemmed from his experience of playing in the Number 8 position and was complemented by his willingness to train hard. He sometimes scored, for example in the game between the Neath/Aberavon team and the 1953–4 All Blacks, following a speedy run-in of some 20–30 yards, which was uncommon for a prop in those days. Similarly, against

Ireland in 1955, he burst over the line from some 20 yards
to score his only try for Wales.

Indeed, it was believed that he was the prototype for
the following generation of props, who were required
to be large, strong and quick around the field. Another
distinguishing feature which C C possessed was a rather
pucka English accent which erroneously seemed to imply
that his roots lay somewhere beyond the Neath Valley!
This was doubtless the reason why he was teased with
the title The Duke of Crynant by colleagues at the time.
He learned his early rugby at Neath Grammar School, an
institution renowned for its excellence in nurturing talent

in that particular field. While a pupil there he represented the Welsh Secondary Schools XV and proceeded to study engineering at University College, Cardiff which eventually led him to a senior position at the hot-strip mills of the local steelworks.

CC won the first of his 14 Welsh caps at Murrayfield against Scotland in 1953, and his last at the same venue in 1957. He won his second cap against Bob Stuart's powerful All Black pack and, during his career, fared well against some of the best props in the world at the time. His greatest achievements took place on the British Lions tour to South Africa in 1955. The Springbok pack, and especially their props, were considered to be almost invincible in those days, yet CC frequently got the better of his opposite number. During the famous Lions victory in the third Test at Pretoria, the Lions front row completely outscrummaged their South African opponents and, by the end of the tour, CC had won the complete respect of the strongest scrummaging nation in world rugby.

He appeared in 13 matches in South Africa and in all of the four Test matches he played alongside his two front row colleagues in the Wales team, Bryn Meredith and WO Williams. He only played in one of the last five Lions matches, which was the fourth test, an encounter for which he wasn't fully fit. At that time he was still recovering from a nasty injury which he had incurred during the previous test. In one of many ferocious scrums, he bit through his tongue and the wound required a number of stitches. Unfortunately, because the wound refused to heal properly, it had to be re-stitched on two occasions, causing a painful inconvenience which CC apparently bore with great forbearance.

The team spirit of the 1955 Lions party was renowned and many tales have been told which illustrate both the fun and the playing efforts which formed an intrinsic part of the success of the tour, one of which involved the Welsh front row. Not one of the three, Billy, Bryn or Courtney, spoke Welsh but they were regularly confronted by an opposing front row which took great pride in speaking Afrikans, their native language, in the scrum, thereby hoping to undermine the confidence of the Welsh trio. However Courtney and his two colleagues devised a plan to regain the psychological advantage and to confuse their Afrikaner opponents. They continually addressed the three South Africans with the Welsh equivalent of Good Morning! Good Night! Merry Christmas! and Happy New Year!

DAI MORRIS

WILLIAM DAVID MORRIS hails from Rhigos in the Cynon Valley and it is probably true to say that no Welsh rugby player ever had such strong ties to his native locality than Dai. It is commonly believed that he would have won many more honours in the game were it not for the fact that he suffered from homesickness and always appeared to be pleased to have been left at home by various touring parties. It was a source of considerable surprise to all rugby followers in 1971 that he hadn't been chosen by the British Lions to tour Australia and New Zealand. This was despite the fact that he was at the time one of the star players in the Welsh XV that had just won the Grand Slam and that fourteen members of the squad had been selected for that tour. His playing colleague, John Dawes, offered the following explanation for his omission: "He was never a good traveller, especially when flying was involved. He always went by rail and ferry to venues like Paris and Dublin. I also recall his unease when we were in New Zealand two years earlier, and my guess is that he let it be known that he did not wish to fly to the southern hemisphere again." It is the opinion of most rugby critics that Dai Morris was the finest back row forward never to have represented the British Lions.

During his career he was regularly referred to as 'The Shadow', a name apparently given to him by Clive Rowlands, the Wales coach at the time. It was a reference to the fact that, as a flanker, he would always be on

Gareth Edwards's shoulder to provide support when the Number 9 attempted to drive forward. If the scrum-half happened to be held up, he says that he would always hear the shout of "Gar! Hwp!" behind him, at which point he knew that all he needed to do, was to flick the ball over his shoulder. For Dai, described by Gareth as 'a scrum-half's dream', was always there to receive the ball and either drive forward to gain substantial yardage or willingly take any covering tackle in order to set up a ruck or maul which would enable Gareth to plan another move. Gareth is of course generally recognised as the best rugby player ever, which prompted Clive to pose the provocative question, "If that's true, what did that make his shadow?"

Yet Dai's support work was not confined to his scrum-half, for he never appeared to be more than a metre or so from the ball when playing for Wales, earning him such accolades as 'the ever present Dai Morris' from commentators such as Bill McClaren. According to the renowned Clem Thomas, "he was probably the most 'on the ball' flanker one has seen". He was an excellent reader of the game, with a seemingly instinctive perception of where the next phase of play would materialise. He responded avidly to the demands of back row play at the time by being a continuous constructive force when linking with players around him and displaying remarkable strength and speed at the breakdown, where he would regularly succeed in warding off the opposition while he made the ball available. In that capacity and, as his try scoring ability would indicate, his huge hands were extremely deft at handling the ball. However Clive Rowlands jokingly suggests that Dai's handling skills were seen at their best at an informal sing-song by the Wales team when they visited Wellington in 1969. During a wholesome rendition of 'Calon Lân', *hwyl* seemed to get the better of Clive and his false teeth suddenly shot out of his mouth. Quick as a flash, Dai Morris dived to catch them before they hit the floor in an admirable display of agility, dexterity and damage limitation!

His physical prowess in the face of more bulky opponents was sometimes surprising in that he stood just six feet tall and weighed a little under fifteen stone. His colleague in the Wales back row for so many games, John Taylor, stated that he had never known anyone to pack so much strength into such a slight body. His stamina, too, was remarkable and his tireless covering in the loose, with his long loping stride, which was the result of a consuming dedication to being fit. He was both physically and mentally hard, conditioned in no small measure by the nature of his work underground at the local pit, Tower Colliery, Hirwaun. His tackling, which was in constant demand, was fierce and uncompromising. Gareth Edwards heard him complain just once during his international career, and that was from a sore shoulder as a result of being called upon to tackle incessantly against a rather robust Fijian team. Dai Morris, in the opinion of Barry John, was "probably, pound for pound, the hardest, fittest, toughest rugby player I've ever known".

Having initially played for Rhigos, and then Glynneath, Dai made his first appearance for Neath in March 1963 against Loughborough College. His magnificent career at the Gnoll spanned 13 seasons during which the team was able to thrive on a regular supply of powerful tight forwards, thus enabling Dai to flourish as an attacking Number 8 or flanker, scoring approximately 150 tries. He made his first appearance for Wales as a Number 8 in 1967 against France at Stades Colombes and scored a try, the first of his six international touch-downs, in the next match against England, during which Keith Jarret claimed his record-breaking 21 points. In the following autumn, despite having an excellent game for West Wales against the touring All Blacks, Dai had been dropped from the Welsh team which was to play New Zealand three days later. However he was selected as a flanker for the first Five Nations game the following season, a position he retained in 31 subsequent games for Wales. His last match against England in 1974 brought an end to an illustrious international career. For eighteen of his appearances for his country he was, along with Mervyn Davies and John Taylor, part of the best ever Welsh back row. Despite his aversion to playing in foreign places, he did manage to tour in Argentina, New Zealand, Australia, Fiji and Canada. During the Wales tour to New Zealand in 1969, when the All Blacks inflicted heavy defeats on their visitors, Dai showed that he was as good as anyone the All Blacks had to offer, and was one of the few Welsh players to return with an enhanced reputation. Similarly, he was one of the few successes in Argentina where an under-strength Wales team lost one Test and drew the other.

After retiring from first-class rugby Dai returned to Rhigos rugby club where he played until well into his fifties. There, he had the pleasure of playing in the same team as his son, and when asked once what his ambition was in life, he answered that it was to play in the same team as his grandson. To the next question, "Well, how old is your grandson now?" he replied "Five months!" There are some who know Dai Morris well who would not dismiss that possibility! His enthusiasm for the game was always unbridled, a fact illustrated by his readiness to appear regularly in celebration and charity matches throughout his career and even in retirement. During his career he would often turn out to play having just completed a shift at the colliery the previous night. Similarily he would usually be the first to arrive at a Sunday morning Welsh squad training session at the Afan Lido in Aberafan, having come there straight from work.

His one other great passion in life has been horses and horse racing. Rumour has it that during certain team-talks in the dressing room, prior to taking the field for Wales, Dai would be listening, by means of a surreptitiously placed earpiece, to an important race at perhaps Kempton Park! In recent years he has had some success as an owner, under trainers such as Tim Vaughan and Andrew Boxhall, with, for example, Helen's Vision, which came first several times at Newbury.

Dai Morris was chosen by the Association of Former Welsh International Rugby Players, in a poll conducted in 2002, as the best blind-side flanker ever to have played for Wales. He was a player who never resorted to dirty tactics, although he was subjected to such play by the opposition on many occasions. He was also considered to be one of the most popular and self-effacing men to have ever worn the red jersey of Wales.

GRAHAM PRICE

G RAHAM PRICE IS widely recognised as one of the best ever tight-head props in the world. During his career as a first-class rugby player, which spanned 22 years, he played over 600 times for Pontypool, won 41 caps for Wales, which was a record for a forward at the time, and represented the British Lions in 12 Test matches. What was even more remarkable concerning those Test appearances was that he played throughout every minute of the twelve games over three successive series in New Zealand and South Africa. That is a record for a Welsh player representing the Lions. It is argued that his success can be attributed to some extent to the fact that, for much of his career, along with Bobby Windsor and Charlie Faulkener, he was part of the remarkable Pontypool front row, affectionately referred to as the 'Viet Gwent' by Max Boyce. But, as noted by W O Williams, another renowned Welsh and British Lions prop, "whenever he [Graham Price] would have played he'd have been outstanding".

His strength in the scrum and his unyielding scrummaging technique, his support work in the line-out, and his fitness and mobility around the field were legendary. He also had handling skills which were alien to most props and was even known to possess a sidestep and a swerve. In the 1983 season, during Pontypool's reign as the most successful Welsh club at that time, he scored six tries, which perhaps was unheard of for a prop! His first try for Wales, in his very first game for his country, was

a testament to his durability and amazing mobility and astounded the world of rugby. He had been chosen, along with his two partners in the Ponty front row, to face France in Paris and spent most of the game providing unyielding resistance to the gruelling efforts of the French pack. Yet in injury time, when Lux, the French centre, dropped the ball, Price hacked it downfield and, accompanied by the sprinter, J J Williams, set off in pursuit. Near the French line he picked it up to touch down for a memorable try and seal an unexpected Welsh victory by 25–10. To run 70 meters at such pace to score was no mean feat, especially for a prop but to do so having been embroiled for eighty minutes in a fierce battle with the French pack displayed remarkable stamina. That try, in a recent poll, was voted the fourth best try ever scored by a Welsh player.

Price attributes much of his success to the influence of his coach at Pontypool, Ray Prosser, who taught him all there was to know about the intricacies of front row play. The coach never allowed his players to get carried away by their achievements and this was amply illustrated when Graham returned to the club a few days after that magnificent victory in Paris. Perhaps he could have expected to receive no little praise for his performance there. However Prosser's reaction was to tell him that in his opinion the French loose-head who had opposed him at Parc des Princes couldn't have been up to much, or Price wouldn't have been able to run 70 meters at the end of the game! Consequently, Prosser made sure that he did extra training that night!

During his career, and in several parts of the world, Graham Price stood up to the worst kind of physical intimidation. He has been recognised as the Welsh player to have received most stitches to head wounds during his career. Bobby Windsor described an incident in New Zealand. "Pricey went down on the ball and the All Blacks' pack drove over him, eight men as one. Nothing new in that, but they liked it so much that they did something which certainly was new: they turned around and went back over him again as if they'd decided they needed a bit of practice. It doubled the number of cuts on Pricey's head." He was also the object of senseless and dangerous gouging. After a game against in France in Cardiff in 1976 his eyes had been targeted to such a degree that he could hardly see. Trying to open one eye was so difficult and painful that he had to go straight home after the game instead of attending the post-match function. He was later informed that the cornea itself had been scratched and it would be a while before he would be able to see properly. Price never named the culprit.

Without doubt the most notorious incident of skulduggery against him occurred on a tour to Australia in 1978. After about five minutes of the second Test between Wales and the Wallabies, the home loose-head, Steve Finnane, ran up behind Price, who was leaving a scrum to go in pursuit of the ball, which was some 30 metres away, and landed a haymaker on his jaw. Finnane already had a reputation as a roughneck and had the nickname of the 'Terminator' amongst his fellow players. However that particular incident was seen all over the world as one of the most cowardly acts of aggression witnessed on a rugby field. Finnane was never again selected for Australia and Price had to be flown home with a badly fractured jaw.

Typically, Graham Price never complained about the incident and even went as far as to try to play it down. "I don't think he set out to do the damage he did, he was just trying to intimidate me. But he caught me coming out of a scrum with my jaw at its most vulnerable – open and gasping for air." In some ways that reaction was a measure of how hard and tough he was. Following a particularly hard battle against the Viet Gwent in the first Test the previous week, Finnane had realised even after only five minutes that he was going to be under the cosh again against Graham Price, whose reputation as a formidable scrummager had preceded him to Australia. Consequently, Finnane decided to 'get his retaliation in first'.

Graham Price always came across as the strong, uncomplaining, silent type. Indeed, Bobby Windsor would teasingly say that when he shared a room with Price, he would be so silent – sometimes for hours on end as he lay on his bed – that you weren't really sure whether he was sleeping or whether he was dead! So, when it came to dealing with rough house antics on the field, Graham could usually be relied upon to do so quietly and efficiently. "You have to stick up for yourself as a forward, especially in the front row. If you let the opposition mess you around they'll get away with murder. As a youngster at Ponty I found it was the law of the jungle and you often had to take matters into you own hands, you have to learn the hard way and stand up for yourself."

He had cause to put this into effect in his second season for Wales when he came up against the French loose-head 'Garth' Cholley for the first time at the Arms Park. He was a 6'3", 17-stone colossus, who in one game laid out four Scottish players and in another punched out three Western Province players in South Africa. He was a player who Graham later described as the most difficult opponent he had played against. In the first scrum of that Cardiff game, Cholley clawed at his face "with such ferocity that I had no choice but to retaliate. With both arms otherwise engaged, my only weapon was my teeth so I sank them into his thumb. Cholley squealed like a stuck pig, and, incredibly complained to the referee" who, in turn, ironically lectured Bobby Windsor for the misdemeanour! Unfortunately, later in the game, Cholley came upon Graham Price from behind in a ruck and clawed once again at his eyes. Price's cornea was scratched and he was forced to leave the field. Later that year Cholley eye-gouged the prop, Gary Knight, who was making his debut for the All Blacks, and tore his eyelid.

Like any good tight-head in that era, Price saw his main task as ensuring a solid square scrum for his forwards, a job which he did admirably throughout his career. However, unlike many other players in that position, he did not see part of his role as helping his hooker with the hooking process. Rather, in doing so, he would concentrate on driving forward and on grinding down his opponents. In those days, the two packs were in contact for a much longer period during a scrum. They would get to grips with each other long before the ball was put in, with the result that such a preliminary encounter was a real test of strength and technique for the two front rows as they grappled to gain superiority. Graham's forte was to take his opponent down as low as possible in the scrum, so that the opposing pack would be unable to gain any advantage, which was within the regulations but which of course could cause problems if lowering the opposition too much would result in the scrum collapsing.

Graham attended West Monmouth Grammar School in Pontypool in his younger days, where he played centre in the junior rugby teams. He was later selected as a prop and represented the Welsh secondary schools rugby team on seven occasions. He was also Welsh champion in the shot and discuss as a schoolboy. He read civil engineering at the University of Wales Institute of Science and Technology and in 2007, he was awarded the CBE (which, according to Charlie Faulkner, really stands for Charlie and Bobby's Efforts!) for services to rugby. He regularly writes a rugby column for a Sunday newspaper and is the Welsh ambassador for SOS IRB Kit Aid, a charity that helps financially disadvantaged youngsters in poor emerging nations to play rugby by providing them with unwanted kit collected in the United Kingdom.

RAY PROSSER

I T WAS SAID of Ray Prosser that he made nails appear as soft as butter. This reflected the reputation he had as a hard, tough player, in the 1950s and early 1960s, with Pontypool, Wales and the British Lions. He also placed great value on such attributes during the time he coached Pontypool between 1969 and 1987, making them one of the most feared and respected teams in the British Isles. His influence on protégés such as Bobby Windsor, Graham Price and Charlie Faulkner was paramount and they, in turn, recognised that they had been coached by the best forwards coach they had ever seen. They would continually praise his intricate knowledge of the mechanics of front row play. In addition, as a result of his demanding, slave-driving training routines, they and their colleagues at Pontypool benefited immensely from Pross's passion for fitness, which emanated from the high standards he had set himself as a player.

For his club Pross generally played in the second row but, like other contemporaries, he was selected for Wales as a prop, on 22 occasions. He first played for Wales in the Five Nations Championship against Scotland in 1956, at the comparatively ripe age of 29, and was selected again later that season against France. In both of these games he played in the tighthead position but won the rest of his caps, as a loosehead prop. He played over 300 games for Pontypool, where he was the cornerstone of the pack. He was physical and uncompromising in his

approach, to the extent that sometimes he appeared over-vigorous, particularly in the line-out, where he was a source of regular possession for his team. He also excelled as a protector, usually in defence of his scrum-half. In the scrum, too, he displayed from the outset the physical and mental prowess required for survival, where players, in those days, he would claim, 'could get away with blue murder'. He also had other essential qualities, such as an abundance of heart and stamina, which were the hallmark of an accomplished tight forward, and a tireless work-rate both in the tight and in the loose.

He was recognised as one of the best props in the British Isles when he was selected to tour Australia and New Zealand with the British Lions in 1958. He became a very popular tourist and was one of the 'characters' of the party. In some ways this was rather surprising, for Pross worked as a bulldozer driver and was one of only three manual workers in the group. Most of the other players held professional positions, with some having come from a public school background. Yet Pross had no difficulty in feeling at home in their company. However, in some ways, the tour proved to be a disappointing experience for Pross.

As was his custom when away from home he suffered badly from homesickness. Indeed it used to be said that he got homesick whenever he travelled anywhere south of Croesyceiliog in his native Monmouthshire, which to some might appear rather an incongruous emotion for such a macho character. Yet the main reason for his disappointment was that he was injured for much of the tour and was able to appear in only 12 of the 31 matches played by the Lions, which included his selection for the final Test of the series against the All Blacks. His troubles started in Australia when he was sidelined with a muscle injury. Worse was to follow in New Zealand where he was laid up with an infected ear (which even led to his hospitalisation in due course) and a badly broken nose. To what extent these injuries were the result of the booting he took from opposing forwards is not clear, but there was no doubt that he had been subjected to his fair share of the rough stuff.

He later made a joke of the fact that, in that final Test, he would go into the scrums 'arse first' so that the All Blacks pack could kick him there instead of in his face! Yet that remark was not uttered as a complaint but rather in acceptance of the fact that it was the lot of forwards in those days to suffer such treatment. To take issue with such ferocity would be to appear to be 'soft', which would have been the ultimate insult for any self-respecting front row forward! Indeed in later years Pross would bemoan the fact that much of the old aggression had disappeared from the game with the result that front row players, in particular, had been deprived of a certain edge that was previously an important facet of their play. At a time when punching, biting and booting were commonplace, survival depended on possessing such an edge.

Prior to that final Test in New Zealand, the Lions had lost the three previous matches in the series. Pross's selection for that match, which was played before a record crowd for New Zealand of 63,000, brought a certain solidity and fire to the Lions pack. They won the game by 9–6, scoring three tries (a try being only worth three points in those days) to a penalty goal by the opposition. Pross more than held his own against the All Blacks' front row, as he also succeeded in doing against Australia and South Africa at various stages of his career.

During his periods of inactivity, due to injury in New Zealand, Pross used his time to positive effect. He undertook a detailed analysis of the power manifested in the technique of the All Blacks' forward play and, along with his own experiences as a player, compiled for some years a mental dossier of the essential ingredients which a coach would require to build a successful rugby team. Within a few years he had done precisely that. In 1967 he took over as coach of Pontypool, when they were at the foot of the Welsh Championship table, and within two years had made them champions, a feat they accomplished on several occasions.

However, their critics complained that Pontypool were a boring side who regularly resorted to a forward orientated game and that they indulged in over-vigorous and sometimes dirty play. Indeed some clubs, such as Swansea, Llanelli, Newbridge, Orrell, Leicester and London Welsh decided to cancel their fixtures with Pontypool. It was a fact that Pross's pack did resort to brutal tactics at times, but often as a result of the efforts of opponents to illegally prevent its domination, for example, in the scrum. It was also true that, à là All Blacks, their pack would perhaps mercilessly rake any opponent who, in a ruck, would be lying in such a way as to prevent them from clearing the ground for their scrum-half. Supporters of Pontypool would also point out that the team would often score as many points, if not more, in a season than most of the other first-class clubs in Wales, and that some of their three-quarters over the years headed the Welsh try scoring lists. This was despite the fact that Pross apparently considered three-quarters to be prima donnas! There was nevertheless irrefutable evidence, with regard to that particular period in the history of the Pontypool club, that they had in Pross the most successful one-club coach ever to have operated in Britain.

He had a penchant for colourful language, which seemed more in keeping with that of a trooper, and was often credited with a turn of phrase which would have a lasting effect on those who were witness to his remarks. For example it is said that during the Lions tour, he had occasion to mischievously complain to David Marques, the upper-class English second row, who was one of Pross's mates in the party, that "you English public school types are all the same, using big words like 'corrugated' and 'marmalade'!" Graham Price recalls one of his memorable sayings during Pontypool training sessions "Do these sit-ups properly and you'll have muscles on your guts like knots on a navvy's bootlaces!" However, the lasting memory of his involvement with Welsh rugby, in addition to his excellence as a player and coach, will be the warmth and sincerity which he brought to his duties.

BRIAN THOMAS

A S A PLAYER throughout the 1960s, and later as an administrator, this giant of Welsh rugby had almost legendary status, particularly in his native Neath. His path to rugby fame started when he captained the all-conquering grammar school team of his home town from which he was later selected to represent the Welsh Secondary Schools team. He was also academically gifted and won acceptance to Cambridge, where he achieved the rare honour of obtaining three rugby Blues. He represented the university in three successive varsity matches against Oxford between 1960–2 during which he was the bane of a succession of Dark Blue packs. At a young age he became a dominant member of a very powerful Neath eight and following his student days he embarked on a distinguished international career which resulted in his winning 21 caps for his country. He became an essential part of the hard core of a pack which was instrumental in enabling Wales to win, during his period in the team, the Five Nations Championship on four occasions and the Triple Crown in 1965 and 1969.

The importance of possession as a means of dominating play was the maxim towards which Brian strove throughout his career, and he used his 17 stone and 6'4" frame effectively to that end. 'Battling Brian Thomas', as he was frequently described by the press, was a master mauler with remarkable upper body strength, which he would use so forcefully to rip the ball clear. At the front of the line he was a telling jumper and also an expert at spoiling opposition possession. In such tight play he was an excellent support player and was able to use his immense strength to fend off opponents in order to provide his half-backs with clean ball or to carry the ball forward to the next phase. He was another whose presence could be seen to physically shift a maul and often, as pack leader, his uncompromising and aggressive approach gave a particular edge to his team's performance.

He was not known for mobility in the loose and, in that respect, especially when playing for Neath, he was often the butt of unkind remarks from partisan supporters of the opposition. In one game at St Helens, for example, a wag from the Swansea Valley was heard to comment "Oi, Thomas! We've got a mountain in Godre'r-graig that moves faster than you!" Whatever was responsible for his physical prowess during his international appearances, it wasn't attributable to his diet on the morning of a match. It is said, that on such occasions, his only meal was the consumption of a pound of grapes! This was probably more acceptable to his team-mates than the pre-match meal preferred by Max Wiltshire, the second row who replaced Brian in the Welsh team during the latter's period in the international wilderness. He always liked to eat a curry before a match and, in the event of the catering facilities during away trips being unable to accommodate his specific culinary taste, Max would carry a packet of Vesta instant curry in his bag!

For sixteen of his appearances in the Welsh jersey, Brian formed an ideal partnership in the second row with Brian Price of Newport. The latter's excellent ball winning capacity was efficiently complemented by the protection and the power provided by his partner, to the extent that he was unofficially described as Brian Price's minder! They first appeared together in the defeat by England in January 1963, when the Neath youngster, at the comparatively tender age of twenty-three, was one of six players making their debut for their country. However, it was in the next game, the win by 6–0 at Murrayfield against Scotland that Brian set out his stall for a lengthy period as a member of the Wales pack. For in that infamously tight game there were 111 line-outs in which Brian excelled with his impressive support work and mauling. The following season, as a member of the combined Neath/Aberavon team, he was put to the test against a formidable New Zealand pack and was not found wanting. Later that season, he was to score his only international try against Scotland, which led to Wales being undefeated at the end of that particular campaign, giving them a share of the championship. During his career he twice played for his country as loose-head prop. On both occasions Wales suffered convincing defeats at the hands of New Zealand but his selection in such a demanding and unaccustomed position, against such a formidable pack, was indicative of his strength and durability.

In the summer of 1963 he was a member of the Wales team that toured South Africa, which was a supreme test of Brian's ability and stamina. For, he played in all five matches there, and in some of the regional games, was commended for his impressive performance. However the one Test match played there resulted in the biggest Welsh defeat in an international match for forty years. The visitors' forwards had been overwhelmed by their counterparts, who, in response to recent law changes to

encourage open play, produced an enthralling display of mobility and handling skills.

During the following season, there was an incident which is said to have had a significant effect on Brian's international career. After the game against England at the Arms Park, which Wales won by 14–3, Geoff Frankcom, the visitors' centre, claimed he had been bitten by a Welsh player. No one owned up to the deed and no individual was censured. The only member of the victorious team to lose his place for the next game was Brian Thomas. Neither was he selected for any of the remaining Welsh international fixtures that season. Although there was no proof that he was the culprit and, despite the fact that he had never been cited as the person responsible, he was constantly maligned in the press for his aggressive play. Many critics considered him to be excessively robust in his approach on the field, and the fact that he was thought, rightly or wrongly, to be no fan of the English, apparently added fuel to the fire.

In that connection Brian Price recalls Thomas's passionate exhortation as pack-leader before the game against England in 1969. "When I shout 'Trevor!' in a Gloucestershire accent, I want you to forget about winning the ball: go through the line-out and trample on Trevor Wintle [who was the England scrum-half] so that when he takes his jersey off at the end of the match it will look as if he's been sunbathing in the Bahamas in a string vest!" Similarly a colleague recalls attending a function many years later at which Brian Thomas was the guest speaker, when he was asked whether it was true that he disliked the English. To which he replied, with tongue in cheek, "Not so! It's just that I haven't eaten a whole one yet!"

His efforts on behalf of Neath during this period were unstinting. He was the lynchpin of a formidable Neath pack that generally swept all before them and in 1966–7, as captain, took them to their seventh championship title. He was renowned as an uncompromising and inspirational leader who would never accept defeat or permit any of his team to do so. He is often remembered for his bloodied and heroic commitment to the cause, which led to many accounts of his unceasing efforts in this respect. It is said that during a local derby against Aberavon, on a particularly stormy day at the Gnoll, he emerged smilingly from a ruck, which had involved most of the two packs, covered in mud and with blood streaming from his mouth. At this point a home supporter is said to have shouted "Aberavon! You'd better count your forwards! I think he's eaten one of you!"

His final achievement in Neath colours was winning the Welsh Cup, on the occasion of its inception, at the end of the 1971–2 season. He then withdrew from the rugby scene for a number of years to concentrate on his career as a metallurgist with the British Steel Corporation but in 1982, he became the first-ever team manager to be appointed by a Welsh club, when he took up such a position at the Gnoll. With vision and application, he restored amongst his players a feeling of pride and a sense of achievement, as he guided them to many honours on the Welsh club scene, and beyond, during the following years. With many from Neath being chosen to represent their country, under Brian's leadership the team favoured a hard but exciting style of rugby, centred on mobile forwards and backs who played with a cutting edge, all of which led to success and admiration for the Neath way.

Brian still valued a robust, physical approach to the game, but never at the expense of the skills that were allowed to flourish as a result.

DELME THOMAS

THERE WILL BE some who might argue with the decision to include Delme in a selection of the hardest players to have represented Wales in the postwar era. In the first instance his quiet, gentle nature was so alien to the aggressive demands of his position in the second row of the pack. Secondly, his work on the field did not overtly display traits which would normally be associated with the 'hard' men. However a former Welsh international succinctly justified his selection with the words, "No second row would be able to win as much clean ball in the line-out as Delme did, during a period in the game when the laws offered little protection to jumpers, unless he was really hard".

A native of Bancyfelin, near Carmarthen he learned his rugby at St Clears Secondary Modern School. In 1961, he was invited to join Llanelli Rugby Club, having been capped for Wales at youth level. He soon adjusted to the physical demands of Welsh club rugby, but at the age of twenty-one, he found himself facing the might of the All Blacks pack when they came to Stradey Park in 1963. He had an impressive game, particularly in the light of the fact that during one period in the match, Llanelli were reduced to six forwards. Following that encounter he realised that if he was to compete in the future against players of that calibre he would have to build himself up physically, so he made a conscious effort to achieve that aim. Even so, when he was in his prime he weighed just 16 stone and was 6'3" tall, which perhaps would not compare with the size of second row players in the modern game.

Delme's talents soon came to the attention of the Welsh selectors but despite gaining selection for four Welsh trials, he couldn't at that time force himself into the team. It was therefore a surprise to him, and to most rugby followers, that he was selected to tour with the Lions in New Zealand in 1966. Delme accepted from the outset that he would be going as the fourth choice second row but after a handful of midweek matches, during which he survived constant and substantial interference and barging, it soon became apparent that he would be a serious contender for a Test place. In due course he was selected as a second row for the second Test, alongside Willie John McBride. This created a precedent, in that Delme was the first postwar player to be selected for a Lions Test match without having been previously capped by his country. What made his choice even more remarkable was that the Lions captain, Mike Campbell-Lamerton, following a disappointing display by the pack in the first Test, was dropped from the team to make way for Delme. It was the first time for some 35 years that a Lions captain had failed to get into the Test team. Yet Delme later made a point of noting that Campbell-Lamerton had been very gracious in the manner in which he accepted his demise, and had wished the Llanelli man well on his debut.

It wasn't long before Delme experienced the extent of the physicality which was such an integral part of All Blacks forward play. Early in the game, standing opposite Colin Meads in the line-out, he jumped to try and claim a throw-in, but suddenly found himself lying on the ground, having lost one of his front teeth, following a Meads 'special'. Yet

Delme recognised that he had no cause for complaint since in earlier line-outs, he had tended to climb all over Meads in trying to compete for the ball. The punch, therefore, was the All Black's way of letting the Welshman know that he was not going to be messed about by a 23-year-old 'rookie'! Nevertheless he put in a commendable performance against the King Country second row, but admitted that the experience was a huge lesson for him. It also left him with an undiminished appreciation of the ruthless style of play which the All Blacks utilised to such good effect, in particular with regard to opponents who found themselves on the wrong side of a ruck.

The Lions lost that game and Campbell-Lamerton regained his place in the second row for the next Test.

However since it was thought that the team could not afford to do without Delme's valuable contribution, particularly in the line-out, he was asked to play tight-head prop. It was testimony to Delme's willingness to serve the team in any way possible and to his versatility and durability that he readily agreed to play in such a demanding and unfamiliar position against probably the most powerful pack in the world. He unfortunately got injured when playing prop in a subsequent midweek match which made him unavailable for selection for the fourth and final Test. That game also ended in defeat for the Lions, which meant they had been whitewashed 4–0. Nevertheless Delme could take pride in his achievements on that first tour and it was evident that an illustrious rugby career lay ahead of him.

Later that year he won his first Welsh cap against Australia at Cardiff Arms Park, as did Barry John and Gerald Davies. However it proved to be rather an inauspicious occasion for the three debutants, as Australia were victorious for the first time ever against Wales. As a result, Delme lost his place in the team to Billy Mainwaring for the next six games. He returned to play against Scotland in 1968 after impressing the selectors when playing for West Wales against the All Blacks. Following two further appearances for Wales in the remaining Five Nations matches, he was selected shortly afterwards to tour South Africa with the British Lions.

It wasn't anticipated that Delme would gain favour over either Willie John McBride or Peter Stagg in the Lions second row but, although he had been chosen as a replacement lock for the first test, he once again displayed his versatility by playing almost the whole of that match as a substitute prop, after coming on in place of the injured

Mike Coulman. He packed down against Mof Myburgh, the celebrated twenty-stone Springbok, who, in the first scrum, lifted his Welsh counterpart clean off his feet and out of the scrum. Delme later admitted that he thought that the giant South African was going to kill him at that point! However, he knuckled down to the job in hand and ensured that he wouldn't suffer such humiliation again. His contribution was such that he was selected as prop for the fourth and final Test when his presence also improved the Lions' performance in the line-outs.

He was once again overlooked by the Welsh selectors for the opening three Home Nations matches of the following season, but returned against England to give one of his most memorable displays in a Wales shirt. He dominated the line-outs to secure the Triple Crown and the Championship, as Wales won by 30–9, with Maurice Richards scoring four tries. However Delme's most memorable game for Wales was against Scotland at Murrayfield in 1971, when, in the final minutes of the match, he secured vital line-out ball, on Scotland's throw, to enable Wales, thanks to a try by Gerald Davies and a remarkable conversion by John Taylor, to win by 19–18 and to proceed to a Grand Slam.

Later that year, Delme was selected for his third Lions tour, to New Zealand. He made 15 appearances out of the 24 games played by the visitors; he was selected for two Tests and came on as a replacement in the final Test. It was fitting that such a fine and willing servant of the game should be there at the end to clinch a historic series victory over the All Blacks. He was of the opinion that playing against the All Blacks in 1966 had been a greater challenge, since at that time their legendary pack contained such established world-class forwards as Whinneray, Lahore, Gray, Meads, Tremain and Nathan. As one would expect from such an honest and fair competitor, Delme was appalled by some of the disgraceful tactics which the Lions encountered on the 1971 tour, particularly in the match against Canterbury. In that game, having come on as a replacement for Sandy Carmichael, who had been cruelly punched off the park, he recalls being kicked on the cheekbone while awaiting a throw-in in the line-out!

Throughout his career Delme was immensely proud of wearing the Scarlet shirt and undoubtedly the experience which he treasured most was leading Llanelli to victory over the All Blacks, by 9–3, in 1972. It was an achievement which Carwyn James, the coach, and Delme had meticulously planned together and it is said that despite being a man of few words, his emotional and passionate exhortation before the team left the dressing room that afternoon had been truly inspirational, with the result that Phil Bennet was in tears when he ran on to the field!

As a person he is quiet, unassuming and liked by all. In the line-out he was a tremendously athletic jumper, able to gain great height due to the immense power he was able to generate from his legs. At times he would get up so high that he was able to take the ball without having to extend his arms above his head. His arms, too, were exceedingly strong, an asset that was undoubtedly developed through his lifetime work as a linesman with the local electricity board. In order to secure uninterrupted possession, he had also perfected a particular technique whereby he would raise his elbows at an angle for protection against barging and interference. His distribution from the line, from his hands or perhaps via the palm or tap-down technique, was generally faultless. His wholehearted efforts on the field were not however confined to the line-out. He contributed with gusto to rucks and mauls, where his talent as a 'ripper' was often evident, and he always added considerable impetus to the scrum.

Delme won 25 caps for Wales and represented the Lions in seven Test matches. For his services to rugby, he was awarded the British Empire Medal by the Queen.

GEOFF WHEEL

ONE OF THE remarkable aspects of the career of Geoffrey Arthur Derek Wheel, or 'Gaffer' as he was known by his colleagues, was that he played rugby for Wales within two years of handling a rugby ball for the first time. Prior to that his first love had been soccer, a sport at which he excelled to such a degree that he regularly represented Swansea City Reserves. However at the age of 21 he joined the Mumbles Club, where his exploits in the second row soon drew the attention of Swansea Rugby Club. Having been persuaded to put his prowess to the test at the highest level at St Helens, he proved to be an instant success. He won a Wales B cap against France in 1973, and was selected the following season for his first full international against Ireland. It was the first of 32 caps for his country, 28 of which were won alongside Alan Martin in one of the most successful second row partnerships ever to have represented Wales.

However there are many who would claim that he was never given the credit he deserved for his wholehearted and invaluable contribution to the Wales pack between 1974–82. He was undoubtedly one of the cornerstones of the team, ensuring an invaluable sense of dependability. He was not renowned for his ball-winning capacity in the line-out, although he was a master of disruption as far as opposition ball was concerned. Very few opponents got the better of him and colleagues recall that he had little difficulty in regularly subduing some of the more

celebrated second rows of his era, such as Bill Beaumont. His work rate and application in the scrum were very impressive, and he was known as a grafter who would readily undertake the more unglamorous facets of tight forward play, with little fuss.

In one particular aspect of such play he reigned supreme. It is generally agreed by supporters, critics and his fellow players that the game has never seen such a masterful mauler, a skill which he perfected by deploying his incredible upper body strength to rip the ball clear, usually from opposition hands. A prominent feature of his efforts, in that connection, was the sight of his blond head continuously bobbing up and down, as the maul literally shook as a result of his fierce application, before he invariably transferred the ball securely to the hands of his scrum-half. In addition, when the opposition seemed guaranteed of possession from a ruck or maul, Geoff Wheel could often be depended upon to wreak havoc in such circumstances.

His achievements in the Welsh jersey earned him wider recognition in 1977. He was chosen to tour Australia and New Zealand by the British Lions, but a medical examination sometime before the squad departed revealed that he had a heart problem which prohibited him from travelling down under. As a result, Moss Keane, the Irish second row took his place on the tour, yet a second medical examination some weeks later, proved the original findings to have been wrong. It appeared that, ironically, he had been deprived of the honour of representing the British Lions because of a false diagnosis. This was perhaps confirmed by the fact that he travelled with the Wales team to Australia the following year with no ill-effects, and played on until 1983 without any indication that his fitness or his health was impaired in any way. It was generally agreed that he fully merited selection for the British Lions tour to South Africa in 1980 but he was inexplicably overlooked by the selectors.

Despite his sterling efforts for Wales over a period of eight years, Geoff Wheel is perhaps more renowned for his part in two of the most unfortunate incidents that have involved the Wales team over the years. Firstly he, along with Willie Duggan of Ireland, was a victim of the first sending-off ever in the International Championship in 1977. Both were dismissed by referee Norman Sanson, after 37 minutes of the match, following some fighting off the ball, a punishment which was subsequently condemned by the public, the press and the home unions for its severity. In the light of numerous, more serious offences that had gone unpunished in the past, the incident in question seemed to be comparatively innocuous. Indeed when referring to the altercation in the *Independent* in 2010, Chris Hewett wrote, "Such was the leniency of officials for much of rugby's history, Hannibal Lecter himself would have been allowed to remain on the field"! As a result, Geoff Wheel was banned for four weeks and his opponent for two weeks. The Welshman's punishment no doubt took into account the fact that he had previously been sent off on a couple of occasions while playing for Swansea. He was undoubtedly a hard and fierce competitor, but did not merit the label of being hot-headed which was sometimes attached to him.

Neither could he be classed as a dirty player. Not that he was averse to making his presence felt, in certain circumstances, with robust action. This is confirmed by Phil Bennet's account of the time he came upon Jean-François Imbernon, the huge French second row, in the bar that he owned in Perpignan. The former outside half had gone to France to report on Llanelli's Heineken Cup match there in 2002. He remembered Imbernon and, for example,

Gerard Cholley, called 'the beast of the Five Nations', as being part of a particularly brutal French pack that tried to physically take him apart during their encounters in the 1970s. During a very pleasant get-together on the occasion in question, Bennet plucked up enough courage to ask his French host why his nose was literally spread over one side of his face. Imbernon smilingly replied that he had caught 'a good one' from Geoff Wheel!

The second unfortunate incident involving Geoff Wheel occurred in 1978, during Wales's match against the All Blacks in Cardiff. Such fixtures have regularly been linked with controversy since their inception in 1905. Yet, most rugby supporters would agree that, with the possible exception of the referee's decision to disallow what would have been an equalising try for the New Zealander, Bob Deans, during that first match, the Andy Hadden 'dive' in that 1978 encounter is generally considered to be the most controversial of all. Wales, who had been the better side throughout, were leading 12–10 with just a few minutes to go, and on course to register a rare victory against the All Blacks. Bobby Windsor threw the ball into a line-out, deep in the Welsh half, in the direction of Geoff Wheel, at which point Andy Hadden, the visitors' second row, shot out of the line as if he had been poleaxed. Such a blatant attempt to feign an offence was evident to almost all in the stadium, since he had made no attempt whatsoever to contest the ball. When the referee, Roger Quittendon, blew his whistle, almost every spectator assumed that he had penalised the cheating All Black. Inexplicably, at the time, the penalty was awarded to the visitors instead, and was successfully kicked by their full-back, Brian McKechnie, to win the match.

It subsequently developed that the referee had penalised Geoff Wheel for employing a lift on the shoulder of Frank Oliver, the other All Black second row, who had not in any event made any attempt to go for the ball and who, it appeared, had backed into Wheel before falling away in an exaggerated manner himself. The referee throughout that match had chosen to ignore all kinds of line-out transgressions by both sides. Yet in the final, crucial moments of the game, he suddenly decided to penalise Geoff Wheel, who had simply held out his arm to fend off any possible interference from Oliver, for a comparatively trivial offence, ignoring such a shameful act as the one committed by Hadden. According to the Wales captain on the day, J P R Williams, even if Quittendon was of the opinion that Geoff Wheel had offended before realising what Hadden had done, he should have reversed the penalty, since ungentlemanly conduct, such as that committed by the All Black, was deemed to be a more serious offence.

There was outrage throughout the country at such a catastrophic mistake by the referee, and, in some quarters, Geoff Wheel was unjustly blamed for his apparent indiscipline at a crucial stage of the game. However subsequent developments confirmed that he had been the innocent victim of All Blacks subterfuge and both Andy Hadden, and the New Zealand captain on the day, Graham Mourie, later confessed that it had been pre-planned ploy, of which all the All Blacks team were aware, to be used if they were 'up against it'. No apology was ever received from New Zealand and no formal complaint was presented by the Welsh rugby authorities. Three years later, on 1 February 1981, the Kiwis cricket team needed to score a six off the last ball of the game to beat Australia in a Test match. At that point, the Australian skipper, Greg Chappell, ordered the bowler, who was his brother, Trevor, to roll that last ball along the ground so that it would be impossible to lift it for a six. There was uproar in New Zealand as a result and Robert Muldoon, the country's Prime Minister no less, referred to the tactic as "the most disgusting incident in the history of cricket, an act of true cowardice"! Ironically, the New Zealand batsman who had to face Trevor Chappell's 'underhand' (in more ways than one!) delivery, was Brian McKechnie, the All Blacks full-back who had kicked the winning penalty following 'the line-out of shame' in 1978! Greg Chappell has never apologised either!

In complete contrast to his controlled aggression and fierce commitment as a second row player, Geoff Wheel was very amiable and good-natured off the field. He was known to be an extremely funny person who liked to indulge himself as a raconteur of jokes and amusing stories, which always went down well with his colleagues. He was a very nervous person before a game and to the annoyance of some of his colleagues would take to making a lot of noise in the dressing room in order to try and assuage his nervousness. He allegedly got so worked up by the *hwyl* of the pre-match team-talk before one particular game, that he ran screaming at the door and head butted a hole clean through it!

Surprisingly, perhaps, he had some phobias which seemed to undermine the accepted image of the 'hard' second row man. He was paranoid about insects, such as spiders, and during Wales's tour to Australia, he was seen late one night hammering a towel to the bottom of the door of his hotel room, lest he be invaded by 'creepy crawlies'! At times he would lock himself in his room and jam up every gap he could find around the door and the windows. He was also terrified of flying, and when returning to Wales after a game against Scotland in 1981, he boarded the plane with a glass of brandy in one hand and a valium tablet in the other, in order that they might help to allay his fears about the forthcoming flight. He unfortunately dropped the tablet and almost tore up the neighbouring seats in his panic to try and retrieve it.

After playing for Swansea in 318 matches, he retired in 1984, having scored 24 tries and having captained the team for two seasons, and undertook coaching duties with the junior members of the club. He is a talented musician and was known to entertain his colleagues on social occasions on the ukelele and the accordion. During his retirement he became organist at All Saints Church at Kilvey in Swansea. He also recently became President of the Gwalia Male Voice Choir in his home town.

During his career as a player he had a number of setbacks, but always came bouncing back and even when he retired he was still regarded as one of the best second rows in British rugby.

J P R WILLIAMS

I N ACCORDANCE WITH the very nature of job descriptions on the rugby field, it was expected that the hard men of any team were generally to be found in the pack. Yet in the light of accepted definitions of such players, it could be argued that some members of the back division also merited their inclusion in this category. However there can be no argument concerning the recognition of John Peter Rhys Williams (known universally as JPR) as one of the hard men of rugby. He was, more importantly, one of the best full-backs ever and, in the opinion of many critics, the best player ever to have appeared in that position. With regard to his reputation as a member of the 'hard brigade', he might well have been inspired by another man of medicine, Dr Jack Mathews, arguably one of the hardest tacklers ever to wear the Welsh jersey. For the first rugby ball JPR ever received, when he was six months old, was a gift from Dr Jack, who was a friend of his father.

At the highest level JPR played for Bridgend, London Welsh, Wales and the British Lions. He combined rugby with his profession as an orthopaedic surgeon and became a consultant in that field. He won 53 caps for his country and was an ever-present member of two Lions sides that were victorious in series against the All Blacks (1971) and South Africa (1974). During his time in the red shirt of his country, he won six Triple Crowns and three Grand Slams. He also had the enviable record of having played against England twelve times without ever losing. He was indeed a very skilful player, displaying, in addition, talents such as speed, agility and vision. In his early years, these attributes led to his excelling also at another sport, namely the comparatively genteel world of tennis. Indeed in 1966 he won a junior title at Wimbledon by beating the future British Davis Cup player, David Lloyd, in the final.

On the rugby field he was renowned for displaying facets to his game which were indicative of being 'hard'. Under the high ball he was unflinchingly rock solid. In addition to unfailingly fielding such kicks, he would always be on the lookout for an immediate counter attack, which would often catch his opponents off-balance, both literally and metaphorically speaking. His commitment in the tackle was total and his timing impeccable. So much so, that it didn't usually suffice to bring an opponent down, but rather to knock him back. If games became physical, he was prepared to 'mix it' with the best and biggest of them all! In addition, his frequent disregard for his own wellbeing on the field, often illustrated by the flow of blood from various parts of his anatomy, enhanced his reputation as a 'hard man'.

In attack his cavalier style of running and his ability to ward off tacklers paid handsome dividends. In that respect who can forget his invaluable contribution to the 'best try ever', scored by Gareth Edwards for the Barbarians against the All Blacks in 1973. JPR not only succeeded in withstanding the illegal high tackle of Bryan Williams during the early stages of the play in question, but also got the ball away efficiently to John Pullin, so that the move could continue.

Many critics, pundits and fellow players have

commented on the 'hard' elements of his game. According to Gerald Davies, his commitment 'bordered on the frightening'! Carwyn James described JPR as being like a forest animal blessed with the sixth sense for the presence of danger, an element which he often sought and loved. To John Dawes he was brave, committed and totally uncompromising. Tim Glover, writing in the *Independent*, was of the view that 'no doctor has played rugby with such wilful disregard for his own well-being since JPR Williams, complete with bloodied headband, was charging around Cardiff Arms Park like a wounded bison'. Indeed JPR himself recognised the dichotomy of his exploits on the rugby field and his calling as a doctor when he said, "I spent half my life breaking bones on the rugby field, then the other half putting them back together again in the operating theatre!"

Specific references to JPR's heroic characteristics are now part of rugby folk lore. One of the great examples of his 'do or die' tackling prowess occurred when Wales played France at the Arms Park in 1976. Wales were leading by six points, with a few minutes to go, when the well-built French winger, Jean-François Gourdon, with the ball in hand, seemingly had a clear path to the Welsh line. At the very last moment, just when he was about to cross, he was hit by a red flash, knocking him some two or three yards into touch. JPR had struck again! Imprinted on the memory of so many Welsh supporters to this day is the picture of him standing in touch for a second, triumphantly brandishing clenched fists, with the stunned French winger prostrate at his feet.

His reputation as a rampaging hero was often enhanced by his bloodied appearances. One of the most dramatic examples occurred when he captained Bridgend against the All Blacks in 1978. During the first half he found himself at the bottom of a ruck on the opponents' twenty-two metre line, with his head sticking out, some five yards away from the ball. One of the New Zealand props, John Ashworth, saw this as a good opportunity to viciously rake JPR's face twice with his studs. As a result, his facial artery was severed and he was left with a hole in his cheek, all the way through to his tongue. Blood poured from the wound, but before he allowed himself to be taken off the field for treatment, he insisted on issuing instructions to the team as to how they should proceed in his absence. When finally he got to the dressing room, it took thirty stitches to repair the damage to his face. The incident had resulted in his losing two pints of blood but, against medical advice, he insisted on rejoining the fray. Bridgend lost 17–6, after a stirring performance, having been doubtlessly inspired by the example of their skipper.

According to Carwyn James "A lesser mortal would never have returned to the field of play. Characteristically, he did."

Two years previously, on a more successful occasion at Twickenham, J P R had once again been the bloodied hero, as Wales beat England to begin their Grand Slam campaign. The week before, when playing for London Welsh, J P R received eight stitches over his right eye. At Twickenham he sustained a cut under his left eye from which the blood poured as he crossed for his second try of the match. He was given stitches after the game but apparently continued to bleed for hours afterwards! Fortunately expert medical assistance was usually available to treat such injuries during a game, but J P R was even known to have stitched his own eye wound during half-time!

His heroism sometimes extended to helping team-mates during times of crisis on the field. During the Lions tour to South Africa, the physical intimidation and transgressions of the Springboks led Willie John McBride to adopt the '99' war cry. This was the call for each Lions player, when a colleague was being put upon by the opposition, to wade into the action, so that no individual would be left isolated. This plan was based on the premise that so many players from both sides would consequently be fighting that the referee would be unable to send them off. It certainly served to inform the Springboks that the Lions would not tolerate any of their bullying tactics. During the third Test it had to be used on more than one occasion.

For example, following an incident when Bobby Windsor was set upon by a particularly big 'Bok, a brawl erupted, with players throwing punches in all directions.

Not to be left out JPR was seen to run some forty metres to join the fray, during which he floored Johannes 'Moaner' Van Heerden, probably the biggest Springbok on the field. The South African later confessed that it was the best punch he'd ever had to take! Some years afterwards, both players met on a train from London to Cardiff, but JPR had to admit that at the time he hadn't recognised his fighting opponent!

Further proof that JPR could mix it with the best of them may be found in the fact that for the last Test during the Wales tour to Australia in 1978, JPR was actually selected to play in the pack. Admittedly, his appearance as flanker had been forced upon the selectors because so many forwards had been injured during the tour. Nevertheless the converted full-back gave a very good account of himself and really enjoyed the experience. For a time afterwards, amongst the lads of the tour party, JPR was called 'Jean Pierre', after Jean-Pierre Rives and the Number 7 Wales shirt he wore that day took pride of place in his jersey collection.

After retiring from first-class rugby he played, until the age of 54, as a flanker for Tondu Thirds, in itself further proof of his durability. He is currently president of the Bridgend Ravens Rugby Club, sings in two male voice choirs and is actively engaged in learning Welsh.

R H WILLIAMS

RHYS HAYDN WILLIAMS, who was affectionately known as 'R H' throughout his rugby career, was described in the press after Wales's stirring victory against England by 5–0 in 1959, as being 'a terrible sight to see'. This was a reflection of the vigorous and uncompromising approach that he brought to forward play in general, and to line-out activities in particular, throughout his career. In addition, the importance of his ball-winning capacity was more than aptly illustrated in that very match. For it was as a result of his clean tap-down to Dewi Bebb, who was representing Wales for the first time, that the winger was able to dash over the English line for the only try of the game. It is also ironic perhaps that R H's fierce reputation as a battling second row warrior belied a gentle, genial and much-liked disposition.

Although he was 6'2½" tall, R H, mainly due to his tendency to stoop a little, frequently gave the impression that he was considerably shorter. He would explain that this had come about because he found himself speaking so often to people of smaller stature than himself, and therefore needed to bring himself down to their level! He claimed that he was in fact 6'4" tall! Notwithstanding this apparent disadvantage he used his height and his 16 stone in weight to excellent effect against the sternest opposition. A little before his emergence at the highest level, the line-out laws had been changed, with the result that jumpers were no longer given the protection of blockers that they had formerly enjoyed. Survivors would henceforth be required to look after themselves and resort to a greater degree of physicality and know-how to ensure clean possession. RH revelled in such conditions.

A native of Cwmllynfell, at the head of the Swansea Valley, RH started playing rugby at Ystalyfera Grammar School and at his village rugby club. He studied for a science degree at University College, Cardiff and represented the college team. After making an impression in a match against Pontyberem in the Gwendaraeth Valley, he was invited to join Llanelli and made his debut for them during the 1949–50 season, at the age of nineteen. Following graduation, he did National Service as an education officer and played rugby for the RAF and the Combined Services teams. He continued to represent Llanelli and during the 1951–2 season, he played on two occasions against the touring Springboks side, firstly for the Scarlets at Stradey Park and then for the Combined Services at Twickenham. Despite being on the losing side on both occasions, RH gave a very good account of himself and was selected for a Welsh trial.

At the time Roy John and Rees Stephens were almost permanent fixtures in the Welsh second row, but RH's progress was noted and eventually rewarded in 1954 when he won his first Welsh cap against Ireland. From then on he was a regular member of the Welsh pack for many years, missing just two of their next 25 matches. He captained Wales in their disappointing performance against England at Twickenham in 1960, when they lost by 14–6. It was a game which was mainly remembered for the impressive debut of Richard Sharp in the outside half position for the home team. It was a notable occasion also in that it was

RH's last appearance for his country. Having been dropped for Wales's next match against Scotland, he decided to retire at the end of the 1959–60 season.

During his tenure in the pack, the Welsh performances weren't particularly memorable, in that just 16 matches were won. Nevertheless R H was invariably deemed to have had an impressive game. He was a good jumper with a particular ability to fend off the obstructive and destructive efforts of his opponents and a readiness to let them know, if there was need, that he was disinclined to tolerate any provocation on their part! He applied himself with notable vigour and fire to the scrums and it used to be said that when R H hit a maul or a ruck it was usually seen to move. He was also considered to be a master of a skill which, although prevalent during that particular period, has long ceased to be a feature of a forward's repertoire, namely the art of dribbling as a means of securing territory and retaining possession. He was never known to have taken a backward step and his stamina and energy appeared inexhaustible. R H was also an intelligent reader of the game, with a knowledgeable appreciation of the requirements of his particular position, and, as a result of his wholehearted commitment on the field, he regularly served as an inspiration to all around him.

On his debut for his country, R H was deemed to have brought a new vigour to the forwards and, by the end of the season, he was dubbed 'the find of the year'. Wales then won five of their next six games, with the pack making such an impression that the front five, along with the flanker Clem Thomas, were all selected to tour South Africa with the British Lions the following

year. It was during that series against the Springboks that R H made his mark as a forward of truly international class, able to stand up to the biggest that South Africa could offer. He played in 15 matches on the tour, including all four Test matches, in which momentous performances by the forwards enabled the Lions to draw the series 2–2. R H excelled in his encounters with the likes of Classens, van Wyk and du Randt, who were considered to be among the best forwards in the world at the time. His performance in the third test, when the seven-man Lions pack held off a rampant opposition to win 23–22, was truly magnificent.

Yet his best was yet to come, in that his record on the Lions tour to Australia and New Zealand in 1959 was superb, despite the fact that the Lions lost the series. He played in 21 matches in all, including six Tests. In the last of the four-match Test series in New Zealand, which the Lions won 9–6, he magnificently claimed the last six line-outs of the game to deny the All Blacks the chance of drawing the match. His stirring performances on that tour, against in particular Tiny Hill and Colin Meads, earned him many accolades. He was named one of the five 'Players of the Year' by the *New Zealand Rugby Almanack*, which referred to him as the outstanding Lions forward of the series. He was also voted the best British forward ever to visit New Zealand and was paid the ultimate compliment by the legendary Meads when he stated that if R H had been born in New Zealand he would have played for the All Blacks. Indeed Meads rated him, along with the Springbok, Johan Claassens, as the two best second rows he had ever played against. The All Blacks' regard and respect for R H was also illustrated by a special invitation he received to attend a farewell party they were giving for Tiny Hill who was retiring at the end of the series.

RH won many other honours as a player, for example being selected to tour Canada and South Africa with the Barbarians, whom he later served as a committee member and selector, and leading the Scarlets on a pioneering rugby-playing visit to Moscow as part of the World Youth Festival Games. He took great pride in representing Llanelli and in particular in his tenure as skipper, especially when they succeeded in defeating arch rivals Swansea on four successive occasions during the 1957–8 season.

After his period in the RAF, he became firstly a research chemist and then production superintendent with the Steel Company of Wales. He nevertheless returned to the field of education administration at the Education Department of Glamorgan County Council in 1970 and in due course became Assistant Education Officer. He served the WRU in an administrative capacity for many years before joining its advisory coaching committee and then becoming a national representative of the Union in 1975. He maintained his interest in the playing side of Union activities by serving as a selector and undertaking managerial duties with the Wales B team on its visit to Spain in 1983. In due course he became the Chairman of the Wales Selection Committee, the Big Five, and in 1991 he would have become President of the WRU. However, due to a controversy that arose when he accepted an invitation to visit South Africa to take part in the South Africa Rugby Board centenary celebrations, he resigned from all WRU administrative duties. He sadly passed away in 1993.

W O WILLIAMS

WILLIAM OWEN GOODING Williams was born 19 November 1929 on the Gower peninsula. From 1949 to 1962 he played for Swansea Rugby Club, mainly in the second row but won all of his 22 caps for Wales as a loose-head prop. He made his name as a tough, powerful member of the pack and possessed a rugged physique which he deployed to great effect, particularly in the tight. He was generally called Billy but also had the nickname of 'Stoker' which surprisingly, perhaps, had nothing to do with his sterling efforts in the boiler house of the scrum, but rather with his duties while serving in the Royal Navy.

Billy was brought up in Gowerton and played soccer until he was 17 years old. He was then approached by the local rugby club and asked to play in the second row, where he made no small impression. Three years after taking up the game, he joined Swansea Rugby Club, where he remained throughout his career. In 1951, at the age of 21 and having had only two years' experience of playing top class rugby, he was selected for Wales. However, since the Welsh selectors were looking to strengthen the pack in readiness for a forthcoming tour by the Springboks, Billy was selected to play in the loose-head prop position against France at Stades Colombes. It was generally assumed that the formidable Neath duo of Roy John and Rees Stephens would form the second row against South Africa, which they did, and continued to do so for the next ten Wales international matches.

There was considerable clamour in the Welsh sporting press at the apparent naivety of the Welsh selectors in choosing such an inexperienced player as WO in the prop position. They argued that there were many loose-head props in Wales who had greater claim to that position in the national side than the untried second row from Swansea. Indeed even Billy himself found it difficult to give credence to the news when he was informed of his selection by his family. He was nevertheless very happy to be in the team and he soon undertook to master his new-found position, spending considerable time and effort in getting to grips with its demands. He rapidly tried to learn the intricacies of front row play which, of course, included the legal, and not so legal (!) tactics which could be employed. That first game ended in a win for France by 8–3, but it was generally agreed that Billy had given a creditable performance.

Indeed, he continued as a member of the Welsh front row for 22 consecutive internationals which was proof in itself of his ability, and versatility too – for between internationals he would revert to his second row position with the All Whites. In December 1951, he played in that position for his club against the Springboks, when Swansea lost 11–3, and opposed them again a week later as prop, this time in the Wales team, for only the second time in his career, in a game which the 'Boks won 6–3. Ironically, the tight-head prop on the day was Don Hayward, who had also been converted from the second row position.

As well as his contests with the South Africans, Billy participated in many other stirring encounters. Perhaps the most memorable was the victory against New Zealand in Cardiff in 1953. The Welsh pack took a battering for most of the game, but showed remarkable resilience to enable the team to be in contention until late in the game, when an inspired cross-kick from Clem Thomas led to Ken Jones crossing for a try which won the match. Once again, a week earlier Billy had put on a rousing display in the second row for Swansea, when they drew 6–6 with the men in black at St Helens. The Welsh hooker for that inspired win against New Zealand, and for the first two years of Billy's time in the national side, was DM Davies, a tough ex-coal miner who had become a policeman in the Somerset force. He must have been impressed with Billy's performance, for he always referred to his rugged loose-head as 'hard boy'!

Following his early primary school days in Gowerton (Billy never had a secondary school education) he took up an apprenticeship at the age of 14 as a boilermaker in Swansea Docks, after which he followed his father, who was also a boilermaker, to the Richard Thomas and Baldwin works in Gowerton. Apart from a period of National Service in the Navy, during which time he played for Devonport Services and the Royal Navy, he remained with RTB until 1959 when the works closed. Following employment for a few years as a steelworker at the Abbey Works he became the full-time convenor of the Boilermakers Union, a position he held for 30 years and which led to his being awarded the British Empire Medal for services to trade unionism.

During his time in first-class rugby it was not uncommon for Billy to work on the Saturday morning before a game and on a Sunday morning following a match. It could be argued that the physical nature of his employment gave him much of the upper body strength that he used so effectively on the rugby field. For it was in the battle of the scrums that Billy excelled. Like every good prop of that era, he saw his task as being primarily concerned with trying to give his hooker an easy ride and with making the opposing front row feel as uncomfortable as possible. On his own team's ball, his efforts would also be concerned with providing solidity and stability. These were duties which Billy admirably displayed throughout his career and which he invariably carried out with a smile.

The ultimate recognition of his talents was his selection for the British Lions party to tour South Africa in 1955, a series which they drew 2–2. Billy was selected to play in every Test match and his wholehearted performances on tour saw him being chosen as vice-captain and pack leader for the third Test in Pretoria, which the Lions won 9–6. For those Test matches, Wales provided the entire front row, with Courtney Meredith and Bryn Meredith completing the trio – a feat not repeated until Gethin Jenkins, Mathew Rees and Adam Jones formed the Lions front row in the second Test in South Africa in 2009. Four props had been selected in that 1955 Lions party, three of whom regularly played tight-head and Billy, by now a loose-head specialist. So Hugh Macleod, the 'Hawick Hardman', one of the best front row forwards ever to represent Scotland and who won 40 caps for his country, was asked to play in the unfamiliar loose-head position. When the tour ended, he paid tribute to the guidance he had received throughout from Billy, which was an illustration of his generosity of spirit whereby he had actively engaged in improving the performance of a competitor for his own position in the Test team.

After a distinguished club and international career W O Williams lost his place in the Welsh team in 1956 following an injury. He was replaced for one game by Rex Richards of Maesteg, who later went to work in Hollywood as a stunt man, and for the next few years by Ray Prosser. He retired from first-class rugby in 1960 and served for many years on the Swansea Rugby Club committee.

BOBBY WINDSOR

OBBY 'THE DUKE' Windsor was generally recognised as one of the best hookers ever, especially by fellow members of the front row fraternity. His former skipper at Pontypool and Wales, Eddie Butler, described him as the best player he had ever played with. He began his career with Whiteheads, the club associated with the steelworks where Bobby worked. He then joined the second-class club, Newport Saracens, and played initially for their third XV before working his way into the first team. He soon came to the attention of Cross Keys, a local first-class club, and was invited to join them in 1970, at the age of 23. A few months later he was asked to attend pre-season trials with Cardiff Rugby Club and, in due course, was selected for the first team for whom he made nine appearances. The inconvenience of having to make four bus journeys between his home in Newport and Cardiff each week, at his own expense, eventually influenced Bobby to return to play for Cross Keys. By the following season, 1972–3, he had been made Captain and in a matter of months he had come to the attention of the Welsh selectors. However, at the end of that season, he joined Pontypool, who had won the Welsh Championship. At Pandy Park he teamed up with Charlie Faulkner, with whom he had played at his three previous Monmouthshire clubs, and Graham Price. At that point the legend of the Viet Gwent was born.

Bobby might possibly have won full international honours sometime earlier than November 1973, had it not been for the fact that, in the first game of the 1972–3 season against Swansea, he had laid out the opposing second row, Mike James, with a haymaker, for which he was sent off and ultimately banned from playing for six weeks. Bearing in mind the aggressive and abrasive style that became associated with Bobby throughout his career, it is perhaps surprising that the James incident led to him getting his marching orders for the first and only time in his career. Following that initial hiccup, he went on to represent Wales in 34 internationals and played 325 times for Pontypool, making his last appearance in 1987.

His greatest asset was his strength, especially in the scrummage. He had a particularly hard edge to his game and was a firm believer in letting the opposition know he was 'around' from the outset. Thanks mainly to the efforts of his coach and mentor at Pontypool, Ray Prosser, Bobby was well schooled in the technicalities of front row play. 'Press' from the outset emphasised the importance of "the position of your feet, position of your body, when to bind, when not to bind. He'd always give you a few options, so that the opposition did this, you did that… You were never stuck." Even though Bobby was a specialist hooker, his knowledge of front row play was such that he often packed down for Pontypool as a loosehead prop and even turned out for the Lions in the tighthead position. In the loose he was extremely mobile and a very strong, balanced runner with a low centre of gravity which made it difficult to bring him down. On the charge he had a talent for bouncing would-be tacklers out of the way and was also an expert in leading the rolling maul to potent effect.

In his day battles between packs were notoriously fierce and the violence which occurred was exacerbated by the

fact that the players who were embroiled in the tight had no protection from match officials. Referees were naturally concerned with watching the ball, while linesmen had no power to intervene if they were witness to any off-the-ball incidents. There were no cameras available to reveal any clandestine foul play and neither were 'fourth' officials employed to confirm such skulduggery. As far as forward play was concerned, it was usually a case of the survival of the hardest and Bobby himself admitted that in the rugby climate of recent years, he would have found it very difficult not to get sent off!

He recalls that the fiercest encounters were invariably against the French, who were mean and vicious to a level he never encountered against any other team. One of his most awesome experiences would be to charge into a scrum from ten feet against 110 stone of French forwards and with some 90 stone of his own forwards behind him. He says that he would sometimes get up from such set pieces feeling as if he'd been caught in a bomb blast. What went on in such scrums was often very nasty, so he had to be nasty himself in order to survive. For example, the French second rows, although not exclusively so, were masters at landing telling blows on the opposing front row, once the two packs had engaged. He learned to counter this practice by releasing his bind on Graham Price, his tighthead prop for most of his career, in order to free his right hand to ensure 'pay back'!

He played against France at international level some ten times and ended every game but one with a broken nose. Yet he confessed that after the game, the French were usually great company and 'good as gold'! He recalls his very first match against them in a B international at the Arms Park in October 1972. Early in the game the scrum collapsed and, as he lay there on the ground, with his arms pinned, the French number eight took a quick look to ensure that the coast was clear and then kicked Bobby in the face. As a result, when he got up he couldn't see out of one eye and the other eye was obstructed because his nose had been broken and pushed out of position so that it affected his vision.

In the corresponding fixture in Toulouse the following season, the French tight-head prop from the outset took to biting Bobby's ear in the scrums. He therefore instructed the Welsh loosehead on the day, Glyn Shaw, to sort the Frenchman out. So, in the next scrum, Shaw let him have a haymaker to the face. Unfortunately the offending prop had Bobby's ear in his mouth at the time and, as he reared up following the punch, he initially took Bobby's ear with him. As a result the wounded hooker was taken off to have sixteen stitches inserted in his ear, but he soon returned, suitably bandaged, to resume the battle!

Bobby was an essential member of the all-conquering Lions team on the tour to South Africa in 1974. He played in all four Test matches and established himself as an extremely able and resilient hooker. The team had been warned from the outset, by the management and senior players who had toured previously in that country, about the dirty, intimidating tactics which the South African teams would employ, particularly in the pack – so Bobby was ready for them. He adopted the basic ruthless philosophy of 'doing it to them before they did it to you'. Indeed, as instructed, in his very first line-out, he 'belted' the opponent standing next to him, thus establishing the pattern for the remainder of the tour.

But being aggressive wasn't enough in itself. Indeed the performance of the Lions pack, particularly in the scrums was phenomenal. The Springboks had always taken pride in their hard image, physical prowess and macho approach in the set pieces and had regularly dominated opponents in those areas. Yet the Lions pack were more than a match for their counterparts and, in the case of the scrum, deployed particular scrummaging skills to gain their superiority. Bobby explained how they nullified the effectiveness of the big men in the South African front row from the very first test. "We took them so low that at times I used my head to hook the ball, which was perfectly legal because there was no law then saying that you had to keep your shoulders above your hips as there is now. On their put-in I didn't bother with the hooker, I'd come across on the opposition tight-head. We shoved Hannes Marias up so high sometimes that if there'd been a spotlight above the scrum, he'd have burnt his arse and been taken to hospital."

Although the Lions lost the Test series against the All Blacks on their next tour in 1977, with Bobby having been selected for the first Test only, their pack once again were the masters of their opponents. As a result, in Bobby's opinion, New Zealand pressurised the law makers to change the rules, arguing that, for example, scrums were too dangerous and a threat to players' safety. The new laws which were consequently adopted no longer permitted the old aggressive techniques and practices, much to Bobby's disgust! He is of the opinion that the lawmakers diluted the physical contests of the forwards to such an extent that rugby henceforth became boring and a game for softees.

Bobby was always a popular figure in rugby circles and known as a streetwise, loveable rogue. He was usually the life and soul of the social life of rugby tours and, in his unofficial role as the joker of the party, his contribution to team morale was invaluable. Yet he experienced more than his fair share of tragedy. His first wife died of cancer at the age of thirty-two and in later years he suffered from depression, following a diagnosis of prostate cancer, and the breakdown of his second marriage, with the result that he actively prepared to commit suicide. However, with the support of his family and friends, he successfully overcame those difficulties and is now enjoying retirement and living in Majorca.

BIBLIOGRAPHY

Phil Bennett, *The Autobiography* (Willow, 2004).

Alun Wyn Bevan, *Straeon o'r Strade* (Gomer, 2004).

Alun Wyn Bevan (ed.), *Grav yn ei Eiriau ei Hun* (Gomer, 2008).

John Billot, *History of Welsh International Rugby* (1970).

Gerald Davies, *An Autobiography* (Allen & Unwin, 1979).

Keith Davies (ed.), *Cofio Grav* (Y Lolfa, 2008).

Edward Donovan et al., *Pontypool's Pride: The Official History of Pontypool Rugby Football Club 1868–1988* (Old Bakehouse Publications, 1988).

Gareth Edwards, *100 Great Rugby Players* (Macmillan, 1987).

Gareth Edwards, *The Autobiography* (Headline, 2000).

Gareth Edwards and Peter Bills, *Tackling Rugby: The Changing World of Professional Rugby* (Headline, 2002).

David Farmer, *The All Whites: The Life and Times of Swansea RFC* (DFPS, 1995).

Scott Gibbs, *Getting Physical: The Autobiography of Scott Gibbs* (Ebury, 2000).

Ray Gravell and Lyn Jones, *Grav* (Gomer, 1986).

Andy Hadden, *Boots'n All!* (Rugby Press, 1983).

Terry Holmes, *My Life in Rugby* (Macmillan, 1988).

Peter Jackson, *Lions of Wales: A Celebration of Welsh Rugby Legends* (Mainstream, 1998).

Royston James, *Can Llwyddiant* (Christopher Davies, 1981).

Garin Jenkins, *In the Eye of the Storm* (Mainstream, 2000).

Barry John and Paul Abbandonato, *The King* (Mainstream, 2000).

Robert Jones, *Raising the Dragon: A Clarion Call to Welsh Rugby* (Virgin, 2001).

R Gerallt Jones (ed.), *Y Gamp Lawn* (Y Lolfa, 1978).

Steve Lewis, *The Priceless Gift: 125 years of Welsh Rugby Captains* (Mainstream, 2006).

Cliff Morgan, *The Autobiography – Beyond the Fields of Play* (Hodder & Stoughton, 1996).

David Parry-Jones, *The Rugby Clubs of Wales* (Hutchison, 1989).

David Parry-Jones, *The Dawes Decades* (Seren, 2005).

Graham Price, *Price of Wales* (Collins Willow, 1984).

Mike Price, *Neath RFC 1945–1996* (The History Press, 2004).

John Reason, *Victorious Lions* (1971)

John Reason and Carwyn James, *The World of Rugby: A History of RU Football* (BBC, 1979).

Huw Richards, *Dragons and All Blacks* (Mainstream, 2004).

Huw Richards, Peter Stead and Gareth Williams (eds), *Heart and Soul* (University of Wales Press, 1998).

Huw Richards, Peter Stead and Gareth Williams (eds), *More Heart and Soul* (University of Wales Press, 1999).

Clive Rowlands and David Farmer (eds), *Giants of Post-War Welsh Rugby* (Malcolm Press, 1990).

Bill Samuel, *Rugby: Body and Soul* (Gomer, 1986).

David B Smith and Gareth W Williams, *Fields of Praise: Official History of the Welsh Rugby Union, 1881–1981* (University of Wales Press, 1981).

John Taylor, *Decade of the Dragon: A Celebration of Welsh Rugby, 1969–79* (Hodder & Stoughton, 1980).

J B G Thomas, *The Lions on Trek* (S Paul, 1956).

J B G Thomas, *The Illustrated History of Welsh Rugby* (Pelham Books, 1980).

J B G Thomas, *Rugger in the Blood: Fifty Years of Rugby Memoirs* (Pelham Books, 1985).

Wayne Thomas, *A Century of Welsh Rugby Players 1880–1980* (Ansells, 1980).

J P R Williams, *J P R: The Autobiography* (Collins, 1979).

Bobby Windsor and Peter Jackson, *The Iron Duke: Bobby Windsor – The Life and Times of a Working-Class Rugby Hero* (Mainstream, 2010).

Hard Men of Welsh Rugby is just one of a
whole range of publications from Y Lolfa.
For a full list of books currently in print,
send now for your free copy of our new
full-colour catalogue. Or simply surf into
our website

www.ylolfa.com

for secure on-line ordering.

TALYBONT CEREDIGION CYMRU SY24 5HE
e-mail ylolfa@ylolfa.com
website www.ylolfa.com
phone (01970) 832 304
fax 832 782